SEC. 17

MICKEY MANTLE

outfield NEW YORK YANKEES

My Favorite Summer 1956

Mickey Mantle

&

Phil Pepe

Island
BOOKS

ISLAND BOOKS
Published by
Dell Publishing
a division of
Bantam Doubleday Dell Publishing Group, Inc.
666 Fifth Avenue
New York, New York 10103

Special thanks to Greer Johnson Enterprises, Inc., of Atlanta.

ISBN: 0-440-21203-0

Reprinted by arrangement with Doubleday

Printed in the United States of America

Published simultaneously in Canada

April 1992

10 9 8 7 6 5 4 3 2 1

OPM

To Billy:

You were the best friend a man could ever have, and you were one of the best managers I ever saw.

I know how much you loved New York City and the New York Yankees.

Thanks for all the good times and the great memories, pard.

We all miss you.

—Mick

The authors wish to thank the many people who helped with the preparation of this book.

To David Gernert for his encouragement and support.

To Basil Kane, who conceived the idea for this book.

To Roy True and Bill Liederman for their friendship and counsel.

To Arthur Richman, Jeff Idelson and the New York Yankees media relations staff for their assistance and the use of their files.

To Mickey's teammates, especially Whitey Ford, Hank Bauer, Bill (Moose) Skowron and Gil McDougald for giving so freely of their time to talk about Mantle in general and the 1956 season in particular.

INTRODUCTION

It was a time of peace and prosperity, a time of the baby boom and the exodus to suburbia. It was 1956. America liked Ike, but it loved Lucy. Huntley and Brinkley teamed up and Martin and Lewis broke up. We the people wondered where the yellow went and wrestled with the burning question "Does she or doesn't she?"

In sports, Rocky Marciano retired as undefeated heavyweight champion of the world and was succeeded by twenty-one-year-old Floyd Patterson, who became the youngest man to win the title when he knocked out the Old Mongoose, Archie Moore. The Olympics were held in Melbourne, Australia. Needles won the Kentucky Derby. The New York Giants beat the Chicago Bears, 47–7, to win the championship of the National Football League. Dr. Cary Middlecoff won the United States Open and the Santos soccer club of Brazil signed a fifteen-year-old called Pelé to his first professional contract. Paul Hornung of Notre Dame won the Heisman Trophy as college football's Player of the Year and Don Larsen pitched the first no-hitter in World Series history, embellishing the achievement by making it a perfect game.

More than 4.5 million readers a week purchased a controversial magazine called *Confidential*, and more than 38 million households had a television set, on which they saw a twenty-one-year-old former truck driver named Elvis Presley make his first appearance on the popular *Ed Sullivan Show*.

Americans also tuned their television sets in faithfully to watch *General Electric Theater*, *The $64,000 Question*, *Gunsmoke*, *I've Got a Secret* and *Dragnet*. At the movies, they stood in line to see Mike Todd's extravaganza, *Around the World in 80 Days*, Cecil B. De Mille's *The Ten Commandments*, Marilyn Monroe in *Bus Stop*,

Frank Sinatra in *The Man with the Golden Arm,* Kim Novak in *Picnic* and Elizabeth Taylor in *Giant.* Elvis had five number one records that year, including his first gold, and on Broadway audiences were enchanted by *My Fair Lady,* amused by *Li'l Abner,* moved by *The Diary of Anne Frank,* and captivated by a spoof called *Damn Yankees.*

And up in the South Bronx, at venerable and stately Yankee Stadium, the renowned "House That Ruth Built," just twenty minutes from Broadway, a real-life Joe Hardy named Mickey Mantle was having the season of his life—thrilling thousands of baseball fans with home runs of such prodigious proportions they were certain he was some fictional character who had sold his soul to the devil.

Only twenty-five years old, with the build of a blacksmith and the boyish good looks of a real-life Li'l Abner, the native of Spavinaw, Oklahoma, in only his sixth season in the major leagues, was already a national hero: one of the most powerful, most dominant, most gifted players in the game.

A future Hall of Famer, legend and true American hero, Mantle would enjoy his greatest success in an injury-plagued career in the 1956 season. He would become the first major-leaguer in nine seasons, only the twelfth player in base-ball history, to win the Triple Crown of hitting (league leader in batting average, home runs and runs batted in) by batting .353 (eight points higher than Boston's Ted Williams), hitting 52 home runs (twenty more than Cleveland's Vic Wertz and the ninth-highest single-season total in history at that time) and driving home 130 runs (two more than Detroit's Al Kaline); and only the fourth player in history to lead the major leagues in home runs, RBIs and batting average in a season. All this in leading the Yankees to their fifth pennant in his six seasons with the team, a nine-game margin over the Cleveland Indians.

Mantle would hit higher than his 1956 average (.365 in 1957) and he would hit more home runs in a single season (54 in 1961), but never again would he put together all phases of his game into one super year as he did in 1956.

"Everything just seemed to go right for me that year," Mantle said. "The big thing was that I was healthy most of the season and everything else just kind of fell in place."

Mantle would continue his success in the World Series, in which the Yankees regained the championship from the Brooklyn Dodgers (the Dodgers had beaten the Yankees the previous year for their first world championship) in seven exciting, heart-palpitating games. He would top off his greatest year with three home runs in seven games and by making an outstanding running catch in center field on a ball hit by Gil Hodges to preserve Don Larsen's perfect game.

He was young, he was at the top of his game and he was a national idol. Mickey Mantle also was a man-about-town in 1956. He was earning the munificent sum of $32,500, which put him in a high income bracket for a man his age, and he lived at the fashionable St. Moritz Hotel in midtown Manhattan. He frequented the most chic supper clubs and rubbed elbows with the famous, not only in sports but in show business as well.

Now, a quarter of a century after he played his final game, Mickey Mantle is more popular than ever. He is recognized wherever he goes. He is in constant demand on the banquet circuit, by television hosts, for baseball card shows, for endorsements. A popular midtown Manhattan restaurant bears his name. He has been immortalized in song. His uniform number 7, long since retired by the Yankees, is a familiar trademark.

Kids who weren't even born when he last hit a baseball know him from bubble-gum cards, from shows, from his television appearances. He is a modern-day Babe Ruth. He has been called "The Last American Hero."

Mickey Mantle comes from a wonderful time in this country when everyday life was much less complicated. It was a time of innocence, of peace and serenity, of simple pleasures and bigger-than-life heroes.

Out of this peaceful time came Mickey Mantle. He was the biggest hero of them all. And he would have his greatest season of a legendary career—as great a season as any professional athlete ever had, anytime, anywhere—in 1956. Mickey Mantle's favorite summer.

—Phil Pepe
Englewood, New Jersey
January 1991

PREFACE

Let me first clear up some possible misunder-standings about my choice of 1956 as my favorite summer. When I say that was my favorite summer, I'm not saying it was my favorite team, or the most enjoyment I ever had, or the best team I ever played on.

I've played on some great teams. When I joined the Yankees in 1951, I joined a great team led by the best all-around player I've ever seen, Joe DiMaggio. They had already won two consecutive world championships and I was happy to be even a small part of winning three more in a row, giving the Yankees a record five consecutive world championships, a record that I feel safe in saying will never be broken. At least not in my lifetime.

The greatest team I ever played on was the 1961 Yankees. Experts have called it one of the greatest teams ever and I have to agree. We had everything—great pitching, outstanding defense, power and depth. If there was one thing we lacked, it might have been overall team speed, but with the hitters we had we wouldn't have used the running game much anyway.

As a team, we hit 240 home runs, a record that still stands. Individually, Roger Maris hit his record 61 homers and I hit 54, so the two of us combined for 115 homers, the most ever by two players on the same team. Moose Skowron hit 28 homers and our three catchers, Yogi Berra, Elston Howard and Johnny Blanchard, combined to hit 64 homers—22 for Yogi, 21 each for Ellie and Blanchard—although Yogi and Johnny played a little outfield and Ellie put in some time at first base that year.

Defensively, I don't know how you could find a better double-play combination than Tony Kubek at short and Bobby Richardson at second. We led the league with 180 double plays and had the best fielding percentage, .980. Clete Boyer was as good a third baseman as I've ever seen, in my mind as good as Brooks Robinson, who many consider the greatest. Ellie Howard catching, Roger Maris in right, Moose Skowron at first, all of them were outstanding at their positions.

Pitching? Whitey Ford won 25 games and lost only 4. Whitey had never before won 20 games, mostly because Casey Stengel didn't believe in pitching him every fourth day. Whitey would pitch every fifth day, sometimes on the sixth and seventh day because Casey liked to hold Whitey out for the good teams. He was such a great clutch pitcher that Casey usually saved him for Cleveland, Chicago and Detroit. Whitey rarely got to pitch against the St. Louis Browns or the Washington Senators or the Philadelphia Athletics, and that's why he never won 20.

When Ralph Houk took over as manager in 1961, he decided to have Whitey pitch every fourth day. Whitey went to Madison Square Garden to watch a basketball game one night during the winter before the 1961 season. Houk was there, too, and they started talking about the team and the prospects for the coming season. That's when Ralph told Whitey he was thinking about pitching him every fourth day that season.

Whitey was so enthusiastic about the idea, Ralph decided to try it, and Whitey wound up winning 25 games.

We also had Bill Stafford, Ralph Terry, Roland Sheldon, Jim Coates and Bud Daley in the rotation, and Luis Arroyo in the bullpen. He was our stopper, although in those days the role of the relief pitcher was not as prominent as it is today. Still, Looey, a little guy from Puerto Rico who had a great screwball and always had a cigar in his mouth (off the field, of course), a smile on his face and a kind word for everybody, won 15 games and saved 29.

We won 109 games that season and beat the Cincinnati Reds in the World Series in five games.

I don't think I ever enjoyed a season as much as 1961. Part of the reason was that I was a veteran, in my eleventh season with the Yankees. Most of the guys who were there when I first came up were gone. Just me and Whitey. We were sort of the team leaders. In fact, Houk came to me in spring training and said he wanted me to be the leader of the team. I never have been the rah-rah type, but I was flattered. I don't know how much leading I did, or how much I had to do, but I had fun.

When I first came up, and for the first four or

five years, I felt like the little brother on the team. There were all these veterans like Joe Collins, Hank Bauer and Gene Woodling. They would tell me to bring them a beer and I was only too happy to do it for them.

By 1961, Whitey and I were the veterans and we became like the big brothers in the family over the next few years. The younger guys would look up to us. But they were different than I was when I first broke in. For example, when Joe Pepitone was a rookie, I would tell him to bring me a beer and Pepi would say, "Get it yourself. And bring me one too."

I guess I was more settled and more secure in 1961, and that's why I had more fun playing baseball than I did in any other year.

Personally, though, I had the best year of my career in 1956. Winning the Triple Crown was the highlight. But perhaps more important, 1956 was the first time I accomplished the things that had been predicted of me, and I finally established myself in the major leagues. And that's why, at least from a personal standpoint, 1956 was my favorite summer.

—Mickey Mantle
Dallas, Texas
January 1991

My

Favorite

Summer

1956

1

"Bums"
No
Longer

⚾

*I*t's Tuesday, October 2, 1956, and I'm in the apartment that I rent during the season at the St. Moritz Hotel on Central Park South, overlooking Central Park in Manhattan. I'm trying to relax, but I can't. It's the night before the first game of the 1956 World Series and I'm really excited. I'm ready to go. The adrenaline is starting to flow.

Playing in a World Series was always special. It always brought excitement, and butterflies in my stomach, but this was something extraspecial. We were going to play the Brooklyn Dodgers.

You had to be around New York in those days to fully appreciate what that meant. There never was a time like that in sports before, and I think I'm safe in saying there never will be a time like that again. Three baseball teams all in the same city—the Dodgers in Brooklyn, the Giants in Manhattan and the Yankees just across the bridge from Manhattan in the Bronx, so close you could see the Polo Grounds, where the Giants played, from Yankee Stadium; you could walk from one stadium to the other.

The rivalry was unbelievably intense among the three teams in those days. It was more intense between the Dodgers and Giants because they both played in the National League and they would meet twenty-four times every season, twelve times in each ballpark. Being in the American League, the Yankees never met the Dodgers or Giants except in exhibition games or the World Series. And that happened quite often.

From 1949 through 1956, two years before the Dodgers and Giants left New York and went to California, at least one of the three New York teams was in the World Series every year. And in six of those years, the World Series was played exclusively in New York—the Yankees against the Dodgers in 1949, 1952, 1953, 1955 and 1956, the Yankees against the Giants in 1951.

If you want to start in 1947 and go through 1958, one of the three New York teams was in the World Series in eleven of those twelve years, and it was played entirely in New York seven of those years. So it was easy to see why kids growing up in New York at that time began to believe that the World Series was their exclusive property. And that's the reason the rivalry among the three teams was so intense.

The excitement at World Series time was at a fever pitch in New York in those days. People used to stand around on street corners, under streetlights, or hang around bars and candy stores just talking baseball for hours. Or should I say arguing baseball? To make those discussions more interesting, and more heated, there were Giant and Yankee fans in Brooklyn, just as there were Giant and Dodger fans in the Bronx.

For hours, they would debate such burning questions as who was the better shortstop, Phil Rizzuto or Pee Wee Reese? Who was the better catcher, Roy Campanella or Yogi Berra? Who was the best center fielder, Duke Snider, Willie Mays or me? The players never got involved in any of that. We respected one another's ability as professionals and, in some cases, we were friends. But the fans sure were serious about it, and very vocal, and often that led to some very heated arguments. I have heard stories of riots, even murders, over baseball arguments in New York.

So that was the atmosphere on the night before Game 1 of the 1956 World Series. Excitement. Passion. Anticipation.

It was even more meaningful for me because I had just completed my best year in the major leagues. I had finally done the things that a lot of people, particularly Casey Stengel, predicted I would do when I first came to the Yankees in 1951.

When I came up, Casey told the writers that I was going to be the next Babe Ruth, Lou Gehrig and Joe DiMaggio all rolled up in one. Casey kept bragging on me and the newspapers kept writing it and, of course, I wasn't what Casey said I was. I don't mind admitting that there was incredible pressure on me because of what Casey was saying, and the fans were expecting so much, which I wasn't able to deliver. I got booed a lot.

And then in 1956, I just put it all together, mainly because I was relatively free of injuries. I led the league in batting average, home runs and RBIs, plus a few other categories. It was my best year, by far. But it wasn't over by a long shot. There was still the World Series to be won. In those days, the Yankees didn't consider it a successful season unless we won the World Series. Playing against the Dodgers made it even more exciting, and it caused me to reflect on how lucky I was.

You see, I consider myself very lucky to have earned my living playing baseball, a game I have loved since I was a kid. Everything I have today, I owe to baseball.

I'm grateful that I played my entire career, eighteen seasons, with one team, the greatest team in baseball history, the New York Yankees. I'm thankful I got to play with such great players, and great guys, as Joe DiMaggio, Phil Rizzuto, Yogi Berra, Roger Maris, Clete Boyer, Moose Skowron, Tony Kubek, Bobby Richardson, Elston Howard and Hank Bauer. And how could I not mention Gene Woodling, Bobby Brown, Gil McDougald and Andy Carey? And the greatest pitching staff I ever played behind that included Vic Raschi, Allie Reynolds and Eddie Lopat?

I know I haven't mentioned them all, but there were so many great guys over eighteen years, it would take practically this whole book to name them all. I loved them all. When I was a young player, they were all like my big brothers. And, of course, there were Whitey Ford and Billy Martin, who really were as close to me as my own brothers. And I was fortunate to play for two outstanding managers, Casey Stengel and Ralph Houk.

I played on twelve American League championship teams and seven world championship teams. I won three Most Valuable Player awards, a batting title, four home-run titles. In 1956, I won the Hickock Belt, given to the outstanding professional athlete of the year, not just in baseball, but all sports. I played in twenty All-Star games and I received the greatest honor a baseball player can get, being elected to the Hall of Fame, in 1974. And that was a special thrill because I entered the Hall of Fame with my pal Whitey Ford, who was the greatest clutch pitcher I've ever seen.

It wasn't all good times, of course. I've known the downside, too. The worst thing was all the injuries I had. I know I could have done better if not for all those injuries, and I've often said, I wish I had taken better care of myself. I would have played longer and been more productive.

When I first got hurt, in an accident that's now pretty famous, I was just nineteen years old.

It was my rookie year and we were playing the Giants in the World Series. I was playing right field and Joe DiMaggio was playing center. In the second game, at Yankee Stadium, there was a fly ball to right center. Either of us could have caught it and I drifted over to get underneath the ball or to back up Joe. All of a sudden, I felt my right knee buckle under me and I fell to the ground. I had stepped in a drainage ditch and tore up the knee. It was the start of what would be a career-long problem with my knees.

I was finished for the Series, which we went on to win in six games. But I was so disappointed because I hadn't contributed to our victory—one single in five at bats.

When you're young, you think you're indestructible. I didn't even do the exercises they gave me to do. I was young and stupid. When you're young and going good, you don't realize all this is going to end. I thought I was going to be a Yankee forever. I figured my legs would just get better by themselves and that was stupid. Today, players take much better care of themselves. They work out all winter, they have Nautilus equipment, plus there's been a lot of medical progress in understanding and treating injuries. I think that's why guys are playing longer. There are a lot of guys playing into their forties now;

look at Nolan Ryan getting a no-hitter at forty-three. I wasn't even thirty-seven when I quit and I know if I had taken better care of myself when I was young, I could have played another three or four years. Maybe longer if we had had the designated hitter in those days.

I had plenty of disappointments in my career, like every other athlete, but two really stand out. The worst was losing the World Series in 1960 to the Pittsburgh Pirates. That was the greatest disappointment of my life because I'm convinced we were a much better team.

Before that, my other big disappointment came in 1955, when we lost the World Series to the Brooklyn Dodgers, four games to three. It wasn't the same as losing to the Pirates five years later. The Dodgers deserved to win; they played well. And it wasn't because we had lost for the first time to our neighbors from across the river that I felt so bad. No, the reason losing that World Series hurt so much was because I had never played on the losing side in a World Series before.

The Yankees won the World Series in 1951, my rookie year, and we won again in 1952 and 1953, beating the Dodgers both times. So I was on a world championship team in each of my first three seasons in the major leagues. Then in

1954 we weren't even in it, so 1955 was the first time I played in a World Series and lost.

The other reason that Series was so disappointing is that I was hurt with a bad leg and managed to play in only three games—two starts, plus one pinch-hit appearance. I had only two hits in ten at bats, one home run and one RBI. Not to take anything away from the Dodgers, who had a great team, but I think if I had been healthy, I could have made a difference.

Still, it was a terrific World Series, even from where I was sitting—mostly on the bench.

We had lost the pennant in 1954 to the Cleveland Indians, who set a record by winning 111 games. We won 103 games, good enough to win most pennants, and still finished eight games behind. That interrupted a streak of five consecutive world championships for the Yankees under Casey Stengel (I was on the team for the last three), and it was assumed we would go right on and make it six, or seven, or eight straight. So, after losing to the Indians in 1954, we came back to win the pennant in 1955, and we were determined to start a new streak and bring the world championship back to Yankee Stadium, where we figured it belonged.

Game 1 of the 1955 World Series was played in Yankee Stadium. Big Don Newcombe started for the Dodgers. He was their ace, with a record of 20–5, and a guy who could really throw hard. I wasn't able to play because of my bad leg and Casey started Irv Noren in center field in my place. As much as I wanted to play, it was probably just as well that I didn't. I never could hit Newcombe, for some reason. But that was all right because the other guys just wore him out, especially Yogi and Joe Collins.

I was very confident in that first game because I knew we'd hit Newk, and because we had my buddy, Whitey Ford, starting for us. Whitey was 18–7 during the regular season, and he always seemed to win the big games for us, and this was a big one. It was important to win the first game of the World Series, especially at home.

The game was a typical Yankees-Dodgers slugfest. Collins hit two homers and drove in three runs and Elston Howard hit a homer. We knocked Newcombe out in the sixth to take a 6–3 lead. The Dodgers got two off Whitey in the eighth, but Bob Grim came in to save it and we won, 6–5.

I sat out the second game too, and again I wasn't needed. Tommy Byrne went all the way on a five-hitter and we won, 4–2. We had played two games and won them both and I hadn't contributed a thing. I guess I wasn't needed, after all. And the newspapers made a big thing out of the fact that never in World Series history had a team come back to win after losing the first two games.

Over in Brooklyn for Game 3 it was a different story. I started in center, then switched to right because Casey wanted to save my legs. I homered with the bases empty in four at bats and we were bombed, 8–3. Talk about not being needed! I miss the first two games and we win. I play the third game and we lose.

Game 4 was almost a carbon copy of Game 3. The Dodgers won by the same score, 8–3. Again I played. Again I got just one hit, a meaningless single, and again we lost. I was beginning to feel like a jinx.

Now the Series was tied, two games apiece, and the Dodgers had the momentum and the confidence. And they pressed their advantage by beating us in the fifth game, 5–3, though they couldn't blame that one on me. Casey benched me for Game 5, also in Brooklyn, and I couldn't fault him. My leg was hurting me and I was hurting the team. Maybe Casey really did think I was a jinx.

All of a sudden, we had our backs to the wall and I was practically helpless. It didn't look like I was going to be able to play any more in the Series, but I was still confident we could win. The sixth and seventh games were to be played in Yankee Stadium and, don't forget, we had beaten them the first two games in our ballpark.

In my place, Casey started Bob Cerv in center field against left-hander Karl Spooner. I felt good about the game because Whitey was pitching for us.

Game 6 was on a Monday. I remember that because the night before, Sunday, Whitey appeared on *The Ed Sullivan Show* and created some controversy. *The Ed Sullivan Show* was one of the top-rated shows on television at that time. Everybody watched it because Sullivan always got the biggest stars in show business to appear. Ed had been a sportswriter in his early years in the newspaper business before becoming a Broadway columnist, then a television host, and he never lost his interest in sports, which were his first love. As a result, he often had athletes on his show, especially before a big fight or horse race or golf tournament or a big game. Nothing was bigger in those days than the World Series, and it was especially exciting, of course, in New York. And since *The Ed Sullivan Show* originated in New York, Ed asked Whitey to make an appearance.

All Whitey expected to do was sit in the audience and stand up and take a bow when Sullivan introduced him. This time Ed threw him a curve. After introducing Whitey, Sullivan asked him a couple of questions about the Series.

"Who's pitching for you?" Sullivan asked Whitey.

"I'm pitching tomorrow in Game Six," Whitey said, "and Tommy Byrne is pitching Game Seven Tuesday."

It was an innocent remark on Whitey's part. What he meant was that Casey had set up the rotation for the final two games—Ford in Game 6, Byrne in Game 7. But, of course, we had to win Game 6 in order for there to be a Game 7, so Whitey should have said, "Byrne's pitching Game Seven *if* we win Game Six." But he never said "if." Whitey had a reputation for being a cocky New Yorker anyway, and this just made him seem cockier.

Naturally, the newspapers made a big thing about it, and so did the Dodgers. But Whitey didn't mind. He just went out and beat them, 5–1, on a four-hitter. We scored all five of our runs in the first inning, Moose Skowron knocking in three of them with a three-run homer, and Whitey just baffled the Dodgers' hitters to let those five runs stand up. There was going to be a

Game 7, just like Whitey said on *The Ed Sullivan Show*. And Tommy Byrne was going to pitch the seventh game for us against Johnny Podres, who had won only 9 games during the regular season but who was almost as cocky as Whitey. He was only twenty-three at the time, but he threw hard and he had beaten us in Game 3, so Walter Alston, the Dodgers' manager, gave Podres the ball for the biggest game of his life.

Once again, the game was going to start with me sitting on the bench, feeling helpless and frustrated.

Game 7 was one of those baseball classics that they'll talk about for as long as there is baseball. From the beginning, it looked like we were going to score a bundle against Podres. It seemed like every time you looked up we had men on base. As it was, we got eight hits and two walks, but we never could get the clutch hit that would finish Podres off.

Meanwhile, the Dodgers scored a run off Byrne in the fourth on Roy Campanella's double and Gil Hodges' single, and Hodges drove in the Dodgers' second run with a sacrifice fly in the sixth. We threatened again in the bottom of the sixth, but we were turned back by one of the most controversial, most memorable plays in World Series history. I'll never forget it. And I was in a good position to see it all unfold in front of me because I had a front-row seat—on the bench.

During their rally in the top of the sixth, the Dodgers sent George Shuba up to pinch-hit for Don Zimmer, who had started at second base. That led to a series of defensive changes in the bottom of the inning that proved to be the turning point of the game, and the Series.

Junior Gilliam, normally an infielder, had started in left field for the Dodgers in an effort to get more batting punch in the lineup. In the bottom of the sixth, with Zimmer out, Alston shifted Gilliam to second base, his normal position. In Gilliam's place in left, Alston sent in Sandy Amoros, a little Cuban who for some reason always had a smile on his face. Sandy could run like the wind and he threw left-handed, meaning he had his glove on his right hand, the one closest to the left-field foul line. Those two facts—Amoros' speed and throwing left-handed—were critical to what happened.

Billy Martin opened the bottom of the sixth with a walk and Gil McDougald followed by laying down a perfect bunt and beating it out. Now we had the tying runs on first and second, nobody out and our best hitters coming up—Yogi, Bauer and Skowron. This was our big chance and I was certain we would win the game right there, mainly because of Yog. He never failed in clutch situations like that.

Sure enough, Yogi hit a twisting drive down the left-field line. When it left the bat I thought, "Sure double, two runs in and Yog on second or third with the go-ahead run," even though Amoros was playing closer to the left-field line than he should have been against a pull hitter like Yogi.

Remember, I said Amoros could run like the wind. He took off and somehow managed to catch up with the ball. How, I'll never know. And he just stuck his glove out and the ball plopped in there. If he was right-handed, with the glove on his left hand, he never would have made the catch, that's how close it was.

To this day, I'm still convinced that Amoros was playing out of position, playing Yogi too close to the left-field line. In all the years I played with Yogi, I don't remember him hitting a ball to left field. Everybody knew Yogi was a dead right-field hitter.

In fact, in the 1960 World Series, I got a lot of attention for a play I made with Yogi at bat. I was on first base and Yogi hit a one-hopper to the first baseman, who grabbed the ball, stepped on first and started to throw to second base for the double play. But instead of taking off for second I dived back to first, so they didn't get the double play. The double play would have ended the inning, but I kept it alive and we went on to score four or five runs and won the game.

Everywhere I go, all over the country, people still remember that play. They had never seen it before, if they weren't from New York, but I hit in front of Yogi for ten years and I knew he was a dead pull hitter. He used to hit one-hoppers to the first baseman all the time, and a lot of times I would dive back to avoid the double play. And that's why I say Amoros was playing out of position. He made a dumb play and it turned out right for him, and the Dodgers.

Making the catch was one thing. How he managed to put on the brakes, stop, turn and throw was another miracle. He probably should have played it safe, not tried to brake and made sure he had made the catch. But he didn't. He gambled and won. Amoros fired the ball to Pee Wee Reese, who relayed to Gil Hodges to double up McDougald at first.

Nobody faulted Gil. There isn't a player in baseball who wouldn't have done exactly what McDougald did—take off as hard as he could when the ball was hit. I know I would have.

Even sitting on the bench, with Amoros and the ball in full view, I never dreamed it was going to be caught. But it was and that took us out of a big inning and cost us the game.

I finally got a chance to hit in the seventh. I pinch-hit for Bob Grim with two outs and nobody on, and I popped up, a fitting sad last at bat for a poor World Series performance on my part.

But after Amoros made that catch, you could see Podres just get tougher. He had new life. We didn't touch him after that and the Dodgers won the game, 2–0, and won their first World Series.

There were no hard feelings in our clubhouse after the game, just disappointment. We respected the Dodgers. They were a great team and they had been frustrated against us in the World Series up to then. We had beaten them in 1941, 1949, 1952 and 1953. Now the Dodgers were world champions and they deserved it.

I didn't feel too bad about it because the Dodgers and Yankees were so evenly matched. If there had been an eighth game, though, I'm certain we would have won and tied the Series.

After the seventh game, nobody in our clubhouse said, "We'll get them next year." Yankees don't talk like that. We just gave the Dodgers the credit they deserved and we looked forward to going to spring training in 1956, having a good year, winning the American League pennant and meeting the Dodgers again in the 1956 World Series.

2

Spring Is Here

*A*fter the World Series, we were scheduled to go to Japan to play a series of games against some Japanese teams. The tour had been booked by the Commissioner's office, I'm sure in antici- pation of us winning another world champion- ship. We weren't too happy about going after losing the Series, but all the arrangements had been made and we had no choice.

I wasn't looking forward to the trip. Merlyn was pregnant with our son David, so she couldn't go, and I wanted to go home and rest my leg. And I was still upset over losing to the Dodgers. The last thing I wanted to do was get on a plane and fly all the way to Japan to play more baseball.

But George Weiss, our general manager, told me I had to go, so I went. I hated it. All the guys had their wives with them except Billy and me. It was all right for about a week. Billy and I did some partying, but, after all, how much saki can you drink? I guess I was a little homesick, because I wanted to get out of there in the worst way. I was ready to come home. But how?

I had a friend, Harold Youngman, who made the trip with me and I got an idea. I had Harold call his office back in the States and arrange for somebody there to send me a telegram saying Merlyn was about to give birth and she was having a difficult time.

It worked. Or so I thought. They let me go home. But this was October and David wasn't born until December, so they eventually found out that I was just making up a story to get out of there. We were supposed to get paid $5,000 apiece for the trip, which was pretty good money in those days. When he found out that my son was born more than two months after I left Japan, Commissioner Ford Frick fined me the $5,000 I was supposed to get paid.

I didn't care about the money. I just wanted to be home. Money never has meant much to me. We never had any when I was a boy, so I figured I didn't need any as a man.

After the 1955 season, the Yankees sent me a contract for $32,500. To me, that was all the money in the world. My dad probably didn't make that much combined all the years he worked in the mines. I didn't even try to get the Yankees to give me more. I just signed the contract and sent it right back. I couldn't wait to go to spring training to get ready for the 1956 season.

It was just about the same team that reported to St. Petersburg, Florida, for spring training in 1956 that had lost the World Series to the Dodgers in 1955. The front office obviously didn't think they needed to make wholesale changes for us to repeat as American League champions and regain the world championship, and we, the players, didn't think so either.

We had a powerful veteran lineup with people like Yogi, Hank Bauer, Gil McDougald, Elston Howard, Moose and Joe Collins; excellent pitching with Whitey, Johnny Kucks, Bob Grim,

Bob Turley, Tommy Byrne, Tom Sturdivant and Don Larsen; and outstanding defense, a Yankee trademark in those days. We were certain all we had to do was stay healthy to bring another world championship to Yankee Stadium.

One new guy we had in camp was a tall, skinny, left-handed-hitting outfielder named Norm Siebern. He wore glasses and he looked like a college professor, but he had a pretty swing and looked like he would be a good hitter. His minor-league record was impressive and the Yankees promoted him to the big club, hoping he might be able to move into left field either full-time or as a platoon player. It was the Yankees' way in those days to keep the nucleus and slowly move in a young player or two each year as the veterans got older. There was no force-feeding, no rushing of young players before they were ready, and the system worked beautifully.

Don't get the idea that we thought we were going to walk away with the pennant in 1956. We knew we were in for a tough fight. Our main rivals figured to be the same teams that battled us the year before when we won the pennant by only three games. That meant our competition would be coming from the Cleveland Indians, Chicago White Sox and Boston Red Sox.

The Indians had that great pitching staff of

Bob Lemon, Early Wynn, Mike Garcia and Herb Score, plus Al Rosen, Vic Wertz and Rocky Colavito to supply the power, and my old teammate, Gene Woodling, as an extra player.

The White Sox were pesky. They'd battle you and scratch for runs any way they could get them. They didn't have much power, but they had guys like Nellie Fox, Luis Aparicio, Jim Rivera and Minnie Minoso, who could slap the ball around and run like hell. And they had pretty good pitchers like Billy Pierce and Dick Donovan.

The Red Sox didn't have the power that season that they used to have, but they still had good hitters, led by Ted Williams, of course. They also had Mickey Vernon, Billy Goodman, Jackie Jensen and Jimmy Piersall.

A lot of people counted the Tigers out, but not me. Not as long as they had Frank Lary, who just had to show up to beat us, and good hitters like Harvey Kuenn and Al Kaline.

Baltimore, Washington and Kansas City weren't going to challenge for the pennant, but I knew it was going to be a tough fight again.

It was hard to believe, but I was about to begin my sixth season with the Yankees—a hardened veteran. It hardly seemed possible. I didn't feel like an old pro. I was only twenty-five.

I could still remember walking into the Yankees' training camp for the first time, carrying my cardboard suitcase and wearing my only pair of blue jeans.

In my first year, 1951, the Yankees trained in Phoenix, Arizona. That was where the New York Giants usually trained, but for some reason, the Yankees and Giants switched training camps that spring. The Giants took our camp in St. Petersburg, and we went to Phoenix.

I remember my first day. I was hitting pepper with a couple of guys and I hit one hard and it went past the fielder and hit one of our players on the shin. I looked up and saw it was Joe DiMaggio. It was the first time I had ever laid eyes on him and here I go and hit him on the shin. I wanted to crawl into a hole in the ground and hide. "Oh my God," I thought. "I've hit my man on the shin. What if I hurt him and he's out of the lineup for a few weeks?" Joe just looked at me and didn't say a word, but I could tell he wasn't hurt. And that's the first time I ever saw the great Joe D.

I was so shy in those days and in awe when I walked into the clubhouse and looked around and saw all those big stars sitting there. Especially DiMaggio. He'd be sitting in front of his locker, drinking a cup of coffee. I couldn't believe I was in the same room with him, much less on the same team.

I remember watching him enter the club-house, all dressed up with a suit and tie, like some dignitary or ambassador. There seemed to be an aura about him. I was too shy and too scared to even speak to him. I don't think I ever said a word to him unless he spoke to me first, which wasn't very often. Joe never was a very talkative fellow. He still isn't, although he's better than he used to be.

To this day, Hank Bauer still reminds me what a hayseed I looked like as a rookie. I showed up for spring training wearing exactly what the well-dressed young man will wear—in Commerce, Oklahoma. I had on these blue jeans which were rolled up at the bottom, and I was wearing white sweat socks and shoes with sponge-rubber soles, a tweed sports coat and a tie that was about twelve inches wide and had a peacock painted on it. I was quite a sight.

Hank was just great to me. He kind of took me under his wing and showed me the ropes in my first year. It was great having Hank as a friend to show me around. He was a veteran who had been a Yankee for about three or four years, and he knew his way around the major leagues. Not only that, he was an ex-Marine and a World War II hero and one of the toughest guys in baseball. Or out. He even looked the part, with a face that somebody once described as looking like a "clenched fist." He wore his hair in a crew cut and he still does. The last of the crew cuts. He looked as tough as he was and he was as tough as he looked. I knew one thing. As long as I was with Hank, nobody was going to mess with me.

Hank was a great competitor and a much better player than he was given credit for. He was underrated because of Stengel platooning him with Gene Woodling. It helped the team, and maybe it helped Bauer and Woodling, but they were such good hitters there was no doubt that both of them could have been full-time players with any other team. Not only full-time players, but stars.

When spring training ended, Hank asked me where I was going to live in New York. I told him I had no plans, that I'd probably live in a hotel, so he asked me if I wanted to room with him and Johnny Hopp. I thought that was nice of him and I accepted.

It was great living with Bauer and Hopp, a couple of old pros. This was 1951 and Hopp had broken into the major leagues in 1939, when I was eight years old. When the Yankees got him during the 1950 season, he was at the end of his career and he was used almost exclusively as a pinch hitter. And what a hell of a pinch hitter he was. He had come over from the National League, where he had batted over .300 twice with the St. Louis Cardinals and once with the Boston Braves, and even though he was at the end of his career he still could hit. He was ideal as a pinch hitter: cool under pressure and a real pro.

Hopp was a genuine old-timer. A throwback. To me, he seemed about as old as my father, and I loved to listen to him and Hank talk baseball. Hopp was like a walking bubble-gum card. He could remember every hit he ever got.

One of the funniest things I ever saw on a baseball field happened to Johnny. He was on first and somebody got a hit and Hopp rounded second and headed for third. Just as he passed second, he pulled a muscle and fell to the ground, but he somehow managed to crawl into third base on all fours. And when he made it there was Frank Crosetti, our third-base coach, waving his arms for Hopp to score!

Hopp was constantly talking baseball with Hank, and even though I never was much for the strategy of the game, I guess something must have rubbed off on me listening to these two vet-

erans. Hopp would always be preaching funda-
mentals, the things Casey taught, like when
you're on second, know how deep the outfielders
are playing so you could score on a single if
they're playing deep or hold up at third if they're
playing close. It was a great experience living
with Bauer and Hopp in my rookie year, and it
really helped me.

We lived in an apartment right over the famous Stage Delicatessen in midtown Manhattan.
We had two bedrooms. Hank and Johnny slept
in one of them in twin beds, and I had the other
one all to myself, but I had to sleep on an Army
cot. I got the cot because I was the rookie, but I
didn't mind. I was just happy not to have to live
in a hotel and to have the company.

That's the way it was back then. If you were
a rookie, you would run errands for the older
guys. You were their gofer. If Hank wanted a
beer after the game, he'd holler to me, "Hey,
Mick, go get me a beer." And I'd go get him a
beer. The same thing carried over to the room.
That's why I ended up with the Army cot.

One of the first things Hank said to me when
we got to New York was: "Hey, Mick, you're in
New York now, not Oklahoma. You can't dress
like that in New York. I'll take you to a place
tomorrow and buy you a suit."

I guess Hank felt pity for me. He took me to this fancy men's store, Eisenberg & Eisenberg, and bought me a sharkskin suit for thirty-five dollars. Hank paid for it. It was the first suit I ever owned and I wore it almost every day.

So I guess I had come a long way by the spring of 1956. Now I was a veteran myself. DiMaggio had retired after the 1951 season and I had taken his place in center field. But not at first. In 1952, we had about four or five center fielders, me, Irv Noren, Jackie Jensen, Bob Cerv. I didn't actually take over center field full-time, where I felt like the position was mine, until about 1953. Even then, I didn't feel I was replacing DiMaggio. Nobody ever will replace DiMaggio.

I guess you can say I felt I was just filling the spot Joe had filled because somebody had to. But as the 1956 season started, my sixth with the Yankees, I still felt like I hadn't done anything special; certainly not like the things Casey had predicted I could do.

I had had a pretty good year in 1955—I led the American League with 37 homers, was first in walks, first in runs scored, tied for first in triples, second in total bases, had a .306 batting average and 99 runs batted in. But I wasn't satisfied. I hadn't achieved what I knew I could and I was determined to start producing in 1956 the way everyone expected me to.

I was especially looking forward to spring training because Billy Martin had missed the previous two springs, serving in the Army. Now we were reunited, the three of us, Billy, Whitey and me, even though we weren't going to be doing too much partying. How much can you party in St. Pete?

Another thing, Whitey and his wife, Joan, and Merlyn and I had decided to bring our kids down that spring and we each took a place out on St. Pete Beach, away from downtown St. Petersburg. Billy stayed at the club hotel, the Soreno. I had stayed there in my first few years and didn't want any part of it.

The Soreno was an old hotel in the heart of the city. You had to wear a coat and tie in the dining room and most of the guests were in their eighties. Or so it seemed. We used to kid Casey that he liked staying there because that's where all his old girlfriends stayed. It might have been all right for an old guy like Casey, but it wasn't the place for me.

Occasionally, Whitey and I would sneak out at night and get together with Billy for a few, but mostly we stayed with our families.

It wasn't the best place for spring training,

especially when we started playing games. We didn't have facilities anything like what they have now, and we had to share a field with the St. Louis Cardinals.

We practiced in one place—Miller Huggins Field—and played our games in another—Al Lang Field.

Miller Huggins Field was nothing more than a huge, open playground, with a baseball diamond and a clubhouse. There were no stands, so that's why we couldn't play our games there. The clubhouse was this old wooden building that didn't even have lockers. You hung your clothes on a nail on the wall in a spot assigned to you.

On game days, we would drive to Miller Huggins in the morning and work out. Then about an hour before game time, we would go by bus, or in our own cars, to Al Lang Field, about six miles away. After the game, we would go back to Miller Huggins to shower and dress. If we had our own cars, we could leave immediately after we were taken out of the game. If not, we had to wait to catch a ride back to Huggins Field.

There were only a few places in St. Petersburg where we could go out at night and, believe me, Whitey, Billy and I hit them all. But, even so, it was a relatively quiet spring in a city in which about 90 percent of the residents were old people who had gone there to retire.

That was all right. The partying could wait until the season started. We were there to get ready for the season and I was looking forward to it because we were determined to avenge the World Series loss to the Dodgers the year before. I was confident we had the team to bring the world championship back to Yankee Stadium.

3

I Like Ike

$\mathcal{W}$e broke camp in St. Petersburg and headed north to start the season, making several stops on the way. In those days, it was customary to stop off on our way home to play games in minor-league towns, either against other major-league teams or against our own farm teams. So we traveled by train, stopping in places like Jacksonville, Florida; Montgomery, Alabama; Chattanooga, Tennessee; and Richmond, Virginia. We played a game in each of those cities.

All of these cities were the same to me. There

was no time to go sight-seeing or to find out anything about the cities. Just get off the train, go to the ballpark, play the game, get back on the train and head for the next city.

Eventually we arrived in Washington, D.C., where we were to open the season against the Senators on Tuesday, April 17.

Opening day is always special. It's a new beginning with all the hopes and promises and dreams of starting from scratch. The adrenaline is flowing, you're excited and everyone's anxious to get the season started after a long, often boring spring training.

When the opening happens to be in Washington, it's extraspecial. The stadium would be full and the game would be attended by lots of politicians.

On this particular day, President Eisenhower was on hand to throw out the first ball. Also there was Joseph Martin, the Minority Leader of the House of Representatives.

Before the game, they announced over the loudspeaker that President Eisenhower was in attendance along with Congressman Martin, and Billy said, "That's my uncle."

I said, "No kidding? How come he didn't come up to the room? Or call you?" I actually believed him. I didn't know any better.

For some reason, I always hit well in Washington, even though it was not a good hitter's park. The fences were deep and the Senators had some good pitchers through the years, like Camilo Pascual and Pedro Ramos.

I wasn't crazy about the city of Washington. For one thing, we stayed at the Shoreham Hotel, way out on the outskirts of town, and there was only one restaurant near the hotel. I just didn't like the city. In fact, I didn't like most of the Eastern cities very much, which had nothing to do with how I hit in those cities. Still, I think it's too bad that Washington doesn't have a team in the major leagues anymore. It is our nation's capital and playing there always was such a thrill for me.

Although the old Griffith Stadium was a tough park to hit homers in, some of my longest and most memorable home runs came in Washington. The one that most people talk about is a ball I hit off Chuck Stobbs in 1954.

Stobbs was a left-hander, which meant I batted right-handed against him, and I always believed I was a better hitter right-handed than left-handed. I hit a ball that went clear out of the ballpark over the bleachers in left field. They said it traveled 565 feet. I don't know about that, but I know I hit it good. Red Patterson, our public relations director, told the writers that he went down and found out where the ball landed and measured the distance and it came to 565 feet. Red got a lot of publicity out of that, which was his job of course, but to tell you the truth, I don't think he ever left the press box.

The other thing I remember about that home run off Stobbs was that Billy Martin was on third base, and when the ball was hit, he went back to the bag to tag up. I used to have this habit when I hit a home run of running around the bases with my head down because I didn't want to show up the pitcher. Now they do high-fives and take curtain calls, but in those days we didn't do that stuff.

So I'm running around the bases with my head down, and when I got near third base, I heard Frank Crosetti, our third-base coach, yelling, "Look out." I look up and there's Billy on third base, tagging up. Here I hit the ball clear out of the ballpark and Billy is tagging up. He was laughing, but I never did let him forget it.

Now it's opening day 1956, and Don Larsen is pitching against Pascual. Our starting lineup had Hank Bauer in right field, Jerry Lumpe at shortstop, me in center, Yogi catching, Moose at first, Billy at second, Elston Howard in left field, Andy Carey at third and Larsen. Lumpe, Billy and Elston were newcomers to our lineup that year. Billy had been in the Army at the start of 1955 and Ellie and Lumpe had been in the minor leagues.

That was the first year players wore batting helmets. But it wasn't a rule; it was optional. The leagues wanted to make it mandatory, but the players turned it down. It was each player's choice and I chose not to wear the helmet. I felt uncomfortable with it on. It bothered me, made me feel like a sissy. It was just a matter of getting used to it, of course, and once I did it didn't bother me anymore.

Wearing helmets is a good thing. It's probably saved a lot of guys from getting seriously hurt, maybe shortening their careers, especially nowadays in the American League. With the designated hitter rule, pitchers in the American League don't have to come to bat, which means if they knock somebody down, they don't have to stand up there and get knocked down themselves. That makes them more courageous, more willing to throw at a hitter.

It seems to me there are more fights in baseball these days. Seems like every time a player gets knocked down, there's a fight. When I played, it was something you just sort of expected and you accepted it when a pitcher knocked you down.

President Eisenhower, who was a big baseball fan and used to go to a lot of games, was going to throw out the first ball of the new season from a box near the Senators' dugout and all the players from both sides went out to try to catch the ball. Whoever caught it would have himself a nice souvenir.

So the President throws out the ball and there's a big scramble and Gil McDougald comes up with it. He brought the ball over to President Eisenhower and asked him to autograph it and the President wrote: TO JOE MCDOUGALD.

I saw Gil recently and asked him if he still had the ball. He said he did. He's saved it all these years, Gil said, because he wants to hand it down to his grandchildren.

I came to bat in the first inning with nobody on. My first at bat of the season and I hit a good one off Pascual, a ball that cleared the center-field wall at the 408-foot sign. The wall was 31 feet high and the ball sailed over the wall and went out of the ballpark, across Fifth Street, and landed on the roof of a building. They said the ball traveled 465 feet. I hoped it was an omen for the season.

In the sixth inning, I came to bat with two

men on and hit my second homer. This one cleared the center-field wall at the 438-foot sign and landed in a clump of trees.

We won the game, 10–4. I hit the two long home runs and made two catches against the center-field wall. It was a pretty good start to what I felt was going to be a good year. I was in the best shape I'd been in since I hurt my leg as a rookie in 1951.

We beat the Senators two out of three in Washington and came home to meet the Boston Red Sox in our home opener on Friday afternoon, April 20. I had been looking forward to the Red Sox series because it was a chance to see Ted Williams hit. He is the greatest hitter I ever saw and I always enjoyed watching him swing the bat, even against us. But Ted didn't play because of a broken blood vessel in his right instep.

Casey held Whitey out of the Washington series because he wanted him to open at home and Whitey pitched a five-hitter and we beat the Red Sox, 7–1. Mayor Wagner was there, but it was a cold day and only fifteen or twenty thousand fans showed up. I hit a three-run homer in the seventh and knocked in another run with a single, but in my last at bat I pulled my thigh muscle running to first when I tried to beat out a drag bunt. I did that a lot back then, bunt for a hit.

When I was feeling good, I would get about twenty or thirty hits a year on bunts and it would help keep me out of any prolonged slumps.

The next day, Casey wanted me to sit out a game and make sure my thigh muscle was completely healed. He was more concerned about it than I was. I told Casey I felt good enough to play. I'm glad I did. We beat the Red Sox, 14–10, in one of those typical Yankee-Red Sox slugfests. I had three hits, including a home run into the upper deck in right field. We hit seven homers in the game. We had played five games and I had 4 homers. Best of all, we had won four of the five.

We swept the Red Sox in three games at Yankee Stadium, outscoring them by a combined margin of 34–17. In the third game of the series, Yogi hit his third homer of the season. I could see that Yogi was going to have another big year. He had belted 27 homers and knocked in 108 runs in 1955, and the way he had started out, it looked like he was going to beat those numbers.

Our big hitter in the third game of the series, though, was Don Larsen, who was a good hitter, especially for a pitcher. I always thought Don could have made it in the major leagues as a hitter. "Goony Bird," as we called him, hit a grand slam and won his second game of the season.

Larsen, in fact, was such a good hitter there were times when Casey would bat him eighth. Tommy Byrne too. One time, Billy took a look at the lineup card taped to the dugout wall and noticed that Larsen was batting eighth and he was batting ninth. Billy got so mad he pulled the card off the wall, turned it upside down and taped it back so it looked like he was leading off.

During spring training, Casey had preached the importance of getting off to a good start. He worked us hard with that goal in mind and it paid off. We were on a roll. After our first seven games, we had six wins and my pal Yogi had 4 homers, tying me for the league lead. Having Yogi hit behind me in the batting order was a big help to me. He was such a dangerous hitter, especially in Yankee Stadium, I knew I wasn't going to get walked too much and I was going to get good pitches to hit.

Ralph Houk did that with me and Roger Maris in 1961. I had always hit third, usually in front of Yogi, but in 1961 Houk came to me and said he wanted me to bat fourth, behind Roger. He said that way Roger would get better pitches to hit. Not to take anything away from Roger, who still had to hit the ball out of the ballpark, but I'm sure it helped him break Babe Ruth's record, having me hit behind him instead of in front of him.

The thing about Yogi that made him so tough was that it was impossible to pitch to him. You couldn't hardly strike him out. They never knew where to pitch him. He'd swing at everything. Balls, strikes, balls almost in the dirt, balls over his head. And he was most dangerous in clutch situations. The Red Sox once brought Mickey McDermott in to face Yogi with the bases loaded. McDermott, who later came to the Yankees and was my teammate, was a left-hander who threw hard but never knew where the ball was going.

It never mattered to Yogi if the pitcher was right-handed or left-handed, if he was a hard thrower or a junk baller, he hit them all. So McDermott comes in and he was wild and the first pitch is over Yogi's head. Yogi just reached up and hit it into the right-field seats for a grand slam.

Now, of course, Yogi is almost as famous for saying funny things as for playing ball. And he did say a lot of weird things, like "It ain't over till it's over" and "I want to thank everybody who made this night necessary." I speak funny too, I guess, with my Oklahoma accent. But not like Yogi. Billy once said Yogi was twenty-one years old before he learned to wave bye-bye.

The funniest Yogi story I ever heard happened one spring training when Billy was the manager and Yogi was one of his coaches. Billy accidentally locked his keys in his new Lincoln Mark VII, and there was no way to get the door open. You couldn't put a wire coat hanger down the window and open the lock, so Billy was very upset. Yogi comes into Billy's office and sees that Billy is pissed, so he asks him what was wrong.

"Aw," Billy said, "I locked my keys in my car and I don't know what to do."

"That's easy," Yogi said. "You gotta get a blacksmith."

One time he was bragging on me to somebody, saying how good I was because I could hit both ways and that I was "amphibious."

He said a lot of things like that and people think he's dumb. But let me tell you, Yogi is dumb like a fox. Not only on the ball field but off the field too.

After the Senators left, the Baltimore Orioles came to town and we just kept rolling. Whitey beat them in the first game of the series with a six-hitter, but I pulled the lateral ligament behind my right knee. Was it going to be another one of those years? I didn't think it was serious. I had learned by now to play with pain and I could tell a serious injury from one that wasn't so bad. Casey wanted me to sit out, but again I insisted on playing. Casey gave in, but when I singled in the eighth inning of the first game of the Baltimore series, Casey had the last word. He sent Billy in to run for me.

Two days later, we started our first road trip of the season. We opened a series in Boston. Most of the major-league teams were flying in those days, but we were still taking the majority of our trips by train. Especially short trips to Washington, Baltimore, Cleveland and Boston. But we'd even take trains to Chicago and Detroit.

The Yankees were one of the last teams that still took sleepers on overnight trips to cities in the Midwest. The reason for that was that our traveling secretary, an old pitcher named Bill McCorry, who had pitched one season for the St. Louis Browns in 1909, was in his seventies and I don't think he trusted airplanes. So whenever we had a trip, Bill would book us on a train. The only time he gave in and had us fly was when it was impossible to get to the city by game time on a train.

I didn't like train travel. Especially the overnight trips. I found it hard to sleep in those little beds. It was very uncomfortable and the noise from the train would keep me awake. I never got a good night's sleep on a train. I preferred to fly. I wanted to get to the next city as quickly as possible. Train travel cut into my party time.

I always liked going to Boston, for several reasons. As I said, any chance to see Ted Williams hit was a thrill for me. Also, the rivalry between the two teams, and their fans, was so strong that the games were fun. Usually high-scoring, which any hitter loves, of course.

One thing I didn't like about Boston was Fenway Park. It never was one of my favorite parks to hit in. I know, the Green Monster in left field is supposed to be paradise for a right-handed hitter, but I never saw it that way. For one thing, the Red Sox had so few left-handed pitchers, I hardly ever got to bat right-handed against them. And right field was a long way away. So was center field. And even on those rare occasions when I did get to bat right-handed, the left-field wall hurt me more than helped me.

To hit one out over the Green Monster, you had to uppercut the ball, which could mess up your swing for weeks. I'm sure I lost more home runs in Fenway Park on line drives that hit the wall, or the fence on top of the wall, than I gained because of the short distance. So as far as I was concerned, you could have Fenway Park. I'd take Griffith Stadium in Washington or Briggs Stadium in Detroit instead.

On our first day in Boston, there was a story in the newspapers that Harvey Kuenn, the Detroit Tigers' great hitter and future American League batting champion, had been called up by his draft board. Before the game, the writers gathered around Casey to get a quote about Kuenn going into the Army.

"Will the Tigers be hurt by losing Kuenn?" one writer asked.

"The Tigers might be hurt," Casey said, "but I'll tell ya one thing, the pitchers all over the league will improve."

My negative feelings about playing in Fenway Park were strengthened in the second game of the series when I hit a home run and didn't get credit for it. I hit a ball to straightaway center field that landed about three or four rows deep and bounced back onto the field. Before the umpires could see where it had landed, Jimmy Piersall, who knew all the tricks and always was a great actor anyway, got the ball and acted like it was in play. He threw it back to the infield. I went into third base, not realizing the ball had gone out of the park. All of a sudden, here comes

Casey out of the dugout, yelling like hell that the ball was in the seats and should be a home run.

Casey lost that argument. He got thrown out of the game, I had to settle for a triple and we lost the game, 6–4.

Also in that game, Ted Williams came to bat and Yogi, who liked to talk to hitters all the time, looked up at him and said, "Hey, Ted, why don't you become a switch hitter?"

Here's the greatest hitter in the history of the game, and Yogi is telling him to become a switch hitter. Ted just looked at Yogi like he was crazy or something. He wasn't the first to give Yogi that look, and he certainly wouldn't be the last.

4

Man-tle
About
Town

*A*pril was a terrific month. We got off to the kind of start Stengel wanted from us. We were 8–3 for the month and in first place, half a game ahead of the Chicago White Sox. And we picked up in May right where we left off in April, with a victory over the Detroit Tigers, Whitey winning his third straight complete game, me hitting my fifth home run. Then we ran into Frank Lary.

Lary was a tough right-hander from Alabama who pitched for the Tigers and was beginning to earn a reputation of being a Yankee killer.

Funny, I thought I hit him pretty good, but he seemed to have most of our guys' number. He did a job on us on May 2, holding us to three hits and beating us, 8–1. One of our hits was my sixth home run, which, coming in the ninth inning, at least saved us the embarrassment of being shut out.

Rocky Marciano was at the game and we had planned to get together for dinner that night. Five days earlier, he had announced his retirement from the ring as the undefeated heavyweight champion of the world. Forty-nine fights, forty-nine victories, forty-three of them by knockout. What a great champion he was.

Rocky was from Brockton, Massachusetts. He wasn't a big guy, shorter than me, but built like a bull. He didn't start fighting professionally until he was twenty-four, which is late for a fighter. He won the heavyweight title at the age of twenty-nine when he knocked out Jersey Joe Walcott in Philadelphia, and he just kept knocking out everybody they put in front of him. He had his last fight on September 21, 1955, when he knocked out Archie Moore. Now he had decided to retire and he came to Yankee Stadium, which I guess was part of his victory tour.

He was introduced to the crowd by Bob Sheppard, the Yankees' public-address announcer, and of course he got a standing ovation.

Although he became a national hero as a fighter, Rocky's first love was baseball. He was a catcher as a kid and a pretty good one. Good enough to sign a contract with the Chicago Cubs and play a little in the minor leagues before deciding to turn to boxing. I often wondered how good a catcher he might have become. With his power and his toughness and his competitiveness, I'm sure he would have made a great backstop, maybe even a Hall of Famer. I could picture him being a lot like Yogi, but a right-handed hitter. But if he had stayed with baseball, the world would have been deprived of one of the greatest fighters who ever lived.

I'm sure it was Rocky's love for baseball that caused us to become good friends. I was living at the St. Moritz, and when Rocky was in New York, he stayed at the Sherry Netherland, which was only a few blocks away. Often when Rocky came to town, the hotel would have big parties for him and I would be invited. That's how I first got to know him. After that, if he was in town, he'd call me and we'd get together for dinner.

When you went to dinner with Rocky, it was like going to a banquet, because he'd always have fifteen or twenty people with him. Not that he needed that many bodyguards, but because he was so popular and so well known, people just wouldn't leave him alone. Also, Rocky enjoyed people and he liked to have his old friends around him. Then there always are going to be the hangers-on who just like to be around professional athletes, especially boxing champions.

There was one time we both happened to attend a press conference at the fancy '21' Club in New York. I don't remember the occasion, but I remember it was a cocktail party and Rocky showed up without a jacket. They won't let you into the '21' Club without a jacket, but the restaurant keeps a supply of jackets for just such situations because they're not going to tell the heavyweight champion of the world that he can't go inside. So they gave him this jacket to wear and it was so tight, and Rocky was so broad in the shoulders, he almost ripped the jacket putting it on.

They had that tiny pickled corn that they serve as an appetizer that looks like miniature corn on the cob and I remember Rocky picking it up and eating the kernels off like you would eat regular corn on the cob, just like Tom Hanks did in the movie *Big*.

They had wooden salad bowls and Rocky would eat salad like he was digging a ditch.

There were about five or six of those plum tomatoes left in the bottom of his bowl, all covered
with oil and vinegar. Rocky couldn't seem to get
the tomatoes on his fork, so he rolled up the
sleeves of his borrowed jacket and picked up the
tomatoes and popped them in his mouth like he
was eating popcorn. And all the oil and vinegar
was dripping down his arm, onto the jacket. He
was funny. I really liked Rocky. I remember
years later hearing that he was killed in a crash
of a private plane in 1969, one day before his
forty-sixth birthday. I hadn't seen him in years,
but I was shocked to hear the news. It was almost like losing a brother.

I enjoyed living at the St. Moritz, which was
one of New York's fancier hotels. We didn't have
anything like it in Commerce, that's for sure. Co-
incidentally, the hotel was located just a few
doors away from where my restaurant is now.

I had a small suite, just a little bigger than a
hotel room. I lived alone, but occasionally Billy
would sleep over on those nights when we would
go out, which happened more than a few times.

Don't get the idea that it was always party,
party, party with Billy and me. We did our share,

but we had quiet times too. We liked to have fun, but that didn't always mean going out and drinking.

We used to like to hang around the clubhouse after a day game. Sometimes we would spend hours there after a game. We had two clubhouse men in those days, Pete Sheehy and Pete Previte. We used to call them "Big Pete" and "Little Pete." They used to take care of the clubhouse, cleaning up after a game, picking up the soiled uniforms, washing them and preparing for the next game.

When we arrived in the clubhouse for a game, there always was a freshly laundered uniform hanging in our locker and our baseball shoes were shined and lined up on the floor of the locker. The two Petes did that and it sometimes took them three or four hours after a game, day or night, to complete their chores.

Pete Sheehy was a wonderful man. He was like a father to all of us. He was one guy who could be trusted with your innermost private secrets. He lived the old slogan: "What you see here, what you hear here, let it stay here, when you leave here."

What stories Pete could tell if he wanted to. But he never did. To anyone.

He had worked for the Yankees for over fifty

years, starting as a kid during Babe Ruth's day. He knew them all. Ruth. Lou Gehrig. Miller Huggins. Joe McCarthy.

Pete and Billy were particularly close. After Billy left the Yankees and went with other teams, as a player and then as a manager, whenever he came back to Yankee Stadium Pete would pay a visit to the visitors' clubhouse to see him. Or if he was too busy to get over personally, he would send Billy a note or a message. And Billy would do the same.

I was sad, a few years ago, when I heard that Big Pete died. But I was happy that somebody had the good sense to honor him and make certain he will always be remembered by naming the clubhouse after him. They have a plaque on the clubhouse door with Pete's picture on it and the words THE PETE SHEEHY CLUBHOUSE. It's the least they could do for such a dedicated and wonderful man.

The clubhouse practically was Pete's home. As I say, he would be there first thing in the morning for a day game and he would still be there, doing his chores, as much as three and four hours after a game.

Many times, Billy and I would just hang around the clubhouse and keep Pete company. I used to like to listen to him tell stories about the Babe and Gehrig and a young DiMaggio.

Billy and I kept water pistols in our locker, and some nights Billy would fill his pistol and begin squirting water at me. Then I would get my pistol and fill it with water and I'd start shooting at him. This would go on for hours. We'd try to hide from one another, taking cover behind a trunk or in a locker and try to ambush each other. These water-pistol fights were a lot of fun. Just like a couple of kids.

The best thing about the St. Moritz was that it was so convenient. I could hop on the subway and get to Yankee Stadium in about twenty minutes. In those days, the subways were clean and safe. And they weren't crowded.

Occasionally, somebody would recognize me and ask for an autograph, but that didn't happen very often. In those days we didn't get the kind of exposure on television that ballplayers get today, so we weren't always recognized. But when we were, people were polite and considerate.

Now you rarely hear about ballplayers riding the subway in New York, but we did it all the time. It was even faster than taking a cab. I remember the first time I took the subway, I got off at the Polo Grounds, which was just across the river from Yankee Stadium, in Manhattan. The sign said BALLPARK, so I got off. I had to walk across the bridge to Yankee Stadium.

Sometimes, on nice days when we had a day game, I would even walk from the St. Moritz to Yankee Stadium. It would take about an hour. I'd walk through Central Park, up through Harlem over the bridge to the Bronx and to the Stadium. Nobody bothered you.

Another thing about living at the St. Moritz, we were right in the center of all the New York nightlife. If we wanted to take advantage of it. And we did. Often.

Once in a while, Whitey would stay in town instead of going home to Long Island to Joan and the kids. Joanie was understanding, but she wasn't *that* understanding, so mostly it was Billy and me.

By now I was no longer a hayseed from Oklahoma. I knew my way around New York and I enjoyed taking advantage of what New York had to offer. I'm not talking about museums, art galleries and theaters. I mean restaurants, bars and clubs.

We might drop in at Toots Shor's, the most famous saloon in the country at the time. It was a hangout for people from show business and sports. Jackie Gleason used to hang out there a lot and so did a lot of athletes. Toots enjoyed having athletes in his "joint," as he called it.

Toots was quite a character, and a pretty good drinker. It was funny to see him and Jackie Gleason get together. Both of them liked to boast and they were always trying to outdo one another.

One afternoon, they were sitting around drinking and they decided to have a race around the block. Picture it, Gleason weighing maybe three hundred pounds and Toots about sixty years old and with a bad hip, and they're going to race around the block.

Toots's place was on Fifty-first Street between Fifth and Sixth avenues. They decided that they would go out the front door together, Toots would head for Fifth Avenue and Jackie for Sixth Avenue. They would go around the block and the first one back at the bar would be the winner. So off they went.

Toots comes back to the bar, huffing and puffing, and there's Gleason, nice and calm, sitting at the bar having a drink.

"What took you so long, pal of mine?" Gleason said.

"How the hell did you get back here so quick?" Toots said.

Gleason just gave him one of those famous know-it-all, cocky smiles of his.

About fifteen minutes passed and it suddenly occurred to Toots that there was something wrong.

"Hey," he said. "How come I never passed you on the street?"

What happened was, Gleason went outside and started running toward Sixth Avenue, while Toots took off toward Fifth Avenue. As soon as he turned the corner, Gleason hailed a cab and had the driver take him back to Toots's place, which is how he made it back long before Toots.

Another place we liked to go was Danny's Hideaway, a restaurant where a lot of actors went. It was Billy's favorite place. We knew the owner, Danny Stradella, and he was also a big baseball fan. One night, I was standing at the bar in Danny's and I started talking to this guy who was standing next to me. It turned out to be Robert Mitchum, the actor. I was surprised how nice a guy he was. I guess because he played so many tough-guy roles in the movies, I expected him to be like that in real life. But he wasn't.

One time we went to Danny's Hideaway for dinner and Danny asked Billy and me if we would pose for a picture with Elizabeth Taylor, her husband, Mike Todd, and Rock Hudson. Elizabeth Taylor and Rock Hudson had just finished making the movie *Giant,* and they had come in for dinner.

Naturally, we agreed. They were very nice and we talked for a little while, then we went to our booth for dinner. All during dinner, Billy kept raving about how beautiful Elizabeth Taylor was. He couldn't stop talking about it. He was driving me crazy.

"Mick," Billy kept saying, "did you see that face? She's the most beautiful woman I've ever seen. What a face."

"Yeah," I agreed, "and did you see that body?"

I hit my seventh homer of the season, and my first right-handed, in a game we lost to the Kansas City Athletics on a game-winning hit by Enos Slaughter. Enos is one of the most remarkable men I ever met in baseball. At the time, he had just turned forty and he was still hustling, still running hard on every ball he hit. He was a great example for young players.

Enos had been one of my first baseball idols.

Where I was raised in northeastern Oklahoma, in the thirties and forties, we didn't have any television, so we used to pick up the Cardinals' games on radio with Harry Caray doing the broadcasts. We were only three hundred miles from St. Louis and my dad, who loved baseball, used to drive me up to St. Louis a couple of times a year to watch the Cardinals play. And Enos Slaughter was one of my favorite players. Enos and Stan Musial.

Slaughter had made a great reputation for himself as a guy who played all out, all the time. A lot of his reputation came from the 1946 World Series between the Cardinals and the Boston Red Sox. After six games, the Series was tied three games apiece, and in the seventh game, in Fenway Park, with the score tied, 1–1, in the top of the eighth, Slaughter singled. There were two outs and Harry (the Hat) Walker hit a single to left center. Slaughter rounded second and headed for third, and everybody expected him to stop there, including the Red Sox. But Enos kept right on running, right through the third-base coach's stop sign. It was such a daring and unexpected move, he took the whole Red Sox team completely by surprise. Their shortstop, Johnny Pesky, never expected Slaughter to keep running, and he just held on to the ball while Enos raced home with what turned out to be the winning run. That one daring play earned Slaughter his reputation for being a hustler and from that day, until he retired from the game, Enos never stopped running.

I remember listening to that World Series game. I was in Children's Hospital in Oklahoma City because my osteomyelitis had flared up. Doctors believed that this bone disease was the result of a high school football injury, and it would weaken my legs for the rest of my life.

I was lucky that penicillin had just come out. For about six weeks, I had to take a shot of penicillin every three hours and it probably saved my legs. Maybe even my life. I don't know if this can be substantiated medically, but I also believe the penicillin helped me grow. I was always small for my age. "Little Mickey" they used to call me. I was fifteen when I went into the hospital and I was so little, my half brother carried me in. But when I left the hospital six weeks later, I had grown so much, gained about twenty or twenty-five pounds, he couldn't carry me out.

I still wasn't enormous. In fact, when I first joined the Yankees, I was only five feet ten inches and about 175 pounds, but I grew to be six feet and my playing weight was 195.

Slaughter had a great career with the Cardinals. He spent thirteen years in St. Louis, then when he was getting older and looked like he was at the end of his career, the Yankees got him in 1954 in a trade for Bill Virdon and a couple of throw-ins and I finally got to meet one of my first baseball heroes. I was surprised at how small he was. He's only about five feet nine inches tall. I thought he was a much bigger man.

Even then, he was still hustling and talking all the time. He hasn't changed. Enos is past seventy now and I still see him once in a while at card shows, old-timers' games and fantasy camps, and he's still hustling and talking all the time. I have a hard time remembering what I had for breakfast, but Enos seems to remember every detail of every game he ever played, all the way back to the 1930s.

In 1955, the Yankees traded Slaughter to the Kansas City Athletics, and now he had come back to hurt us with a big hit.

When I hit two homers in a game against Kansas City early in May it gave me 9 homers in only sixteen games, and for the first time somebody looked it up and found that when Babe Ruth hit his record 60 homers in 1927 he didn't hit his ninth until his twenty-ninth game. That put me thirteen games ahead of Ruth's pace. I was also batting .433 after sixteen games. If I could only stay healthy all year.

Casey bought the beer today. As far back as I can remember, there was always beer in the Yankees' clubhouse. Little Pete used to buy it with his own money and keep it on ice for after the game. He bought soda too and candy bars, and there was always coffee and milk and doughnuts and cake. There was a big cardboard poster with all the guys' names on it, and if you took a beer or a soda or a candy bar, you'd mark it down on the cardboard next to your name. Then at the end of the month, when we got our paycheck, we would settle up with Little Pete, plus a little something extra for a tip.

When we won, Casey would buy the beer, which was no small thing for us. We weren't making much money, so we liked it when the manager paid for the beer. In those days, the manager made more money than most of the players, which shows you how times have changed.

There's still beer in the clubhouses, and soda

and candy bars, just like in our day. The difference is, that stuff is donated. Nobody pays for it. Most baseball teams have beer companies that sponsor their radio broadcasts or their television coverage, and those sponsors just send over a supply of beer.

We never used to have dinner in the clubhouse in my day. If you got hungry, you'd give Little Pete some money and send him to the concession stand for a couple of hot dogs. Later in my career, because there were getting to be more and more night games, there was more food. The reason it started was that a lot of restaurants were closed by the time night games ended, and players had to eat. Also, if they ate in the clubhouse right after the game, they could get to sleep a little earlier.

All we had back then was some luncheon meat and bread. Today, they practically serve a four-course dinner after a game.

We took a doubleheader from the White Sox at Yankee Stadium early in May to take a three-and-a-half-game lead and Casey bought the beer. The newspapers were beginning to write about a Yankee runaway, but we knew it was still early. So much could happen. I wasn't thinking about any runaway. Not yet. Besides, I was hurting too much. I had a knot in my thigh, and one day during batting practice, I slammed a foul ball off my foot. Fortunately, I didn't break any bones, but it sure hurt like hell. Again Casey wanted me to take some time off, but again I convinced him I could play with the pain. I didn't want to sit down now that I had my stroke and things were going so good.

I must have made the right choice, because in a three-game series with the Indians, I hit two more homers, my tenth and eleventh, and I had a three-for-four game and raised my average to .446. But I also cost us a game when I dropped a pop fly by Chico Carrasquel in the ninth inning to let the go-ahead run score, and then Bob Lemon had his good sinker working and beat us, giving the Indians two out of three in the series. My 11 home runs led the American League, but my buddy Yogi was hot on my tail with 10.

Billy hadn't been hitting, and when we lost two out of three to the Indians, Casey benched him and started Bobby Richardson in his place. Knowing what a competitor Billy was, you can understand that he was pissed. The change didn't work. We continued our slide, which reached five losses in seven games. Bob Lemon beat us for the second time in five days and even though I hit my twelfth homer of the season off him, it was no consolation. For the first time in the season, we dropped out of first place and trailed the Indians by percentage points. The White Sox, who had been jockeying with the Indians for second place, slipped to third, just one game out.

One thing you have to say for Stengel, he wasn't the kind of stubborn manager who sticks with a move even if it isn't working. He wasn't afraid to admit his mistake and correct it. The Old Man knew he had to do something to shake us up. We lacked spark. So he put Billy back at second base and he batted Phil Rizzuto ninth, behind Mickey McDermott, which didn't make Scooter very happy. But Billy celebrated his return to the starting lineup by getting three hits. I had been in a mild batting slump and I broke out of it with my thirteenth homer and two singles to get my average back to .400.

All this happened on Billy's twenty-eighth birthday, May 16, and we planned to celebrate after the game. But we were in Cleveland, and how are you going to have a real celebration in Cleveland? So we just went out to dinner and had a few drinks afterward, a mild celebration compared with the one we would have on Billy's twenty-ninth birthday, the following year.

That's when a bunch of us, me, Yogi, Bauer, Whitey and Johnny Kucks, with our wives, and Billy, with his date, decided to have a big bash to celebrate Billy's birthday. It was a Sunday and there was no game the next day, so we planned a big night. We had dinner at Danny's Hideaway, then we all went over to the Copacabana to see Sammy Davis, Jr.

When we got to the Copa, we were sitting next to a bunch of guys who were very loud and rowdy. It turned out to be a couple of bowling teams out on the town, and they were making remarks about Sammy Davis. Hank said something to them, asking them to please quiet down and let us enjoy the show. Soon there were words, and the next thing I knew, we were out in the hall and there was a scuffle. One of their guys wound up on the floor. I thought it was Billy at first, so I picked his head up and when I saw it wasn't Billy, I just dropped him back on the floor.

This guy was lying under a chair and he was all busted up. It looked like Roy Rogers had come rolling through there on his horse Trigger and Trigger had kicked this guy in the face.

The bouncer at the Copa hustled us out of the place and through the kitchen and out onto the street, where we got cabs out of there. The bouncer was trying to protect us. He didn't want us to get in any trouble and have the incident get in the newspapers. But sure enough, the next day when I picked up the paper, there was a big headline that said something like: YANKEES IN COPA FIGHT.

We all got called in by George Weiss, our general manager, and we wound up having to pay for the damage. We even got sued by the guys on the bowling team and we had to go to court. I was really nervous. It was the first time I had ever been in court, and it's still the only time.

I got called on the witness stand and the judge says to me, "Mr. Mantle, are you chewing gum?"

"Yes, Your Honor, I am," I said.

"Well, get rid of it," he said.

I looked around and there was no place to put the gum. No trash can. Nothing. So I took the gum out of my mouth and stuck it under the chair.

We wound up winning the case, but we still had to pay for the damage to the Copa.

Everybody figured it was Billy who slugged the guy who was lying on the floor. He had already picked up his reputation for fighting by then. But it wasn't Billy who hit the guy. I know it wasn't, because I was with him the whole time and I never saw him hit anybody. I don't know who hit the guy, but it wasn't Billy and still he got the blame.

The next day, when I got to the ballpark, there was Billy packing his stuff.

"Billy," I said. "What are you doing?"

"I'm outta here, Mick," he said. "Weiss is going to trade me. He never liked me. He's been waiting for an excuse to trade me and now he's got it."

Billy was right. Weiss was looking for an excuse to trade him. Weiss never liked Billy. He thought he was too brash, not the Yankee type—whatever that means. I always thought the Yankee type was a guy who was a winner, and Billy certainly was that. But Weiss didn't like Billy's fighting and his mouth. And he resented the fact that Billy was Casey's boy. Another reason, I think, was that Bobby Richardson was coming along and I think Weiss figured he would be the team's second baseman for the next ten years.

Bobby eventually took over second base and became one of the best in the game at his position, one of the solid men on that 1961 team that I still believe was the best team I ever played on. Weiss was looking for an excuse to give Bobby a chance to play and to get rid of Billy and now, after the Copa incident, he had his excuse.

It didn't happen right away like Billy thought it would. It happened a month later, on June 15, the trading deadline. We were in Kansas City and Casey called Billy in and told him he was traded to the Athletics. Weiss let it leak to the press that the reason Billy was traded was that he was a bad influence on me and Whitey. Bad influence? At the time Billy was traded, I was hitting around .400 and I had just had my Triple Crown year. Billy was with the Yankees six seasons and, in that time, we won six pennants and five world championships. Do you call that a bad influence?

As Billy used to like to say, "Whitey and Mick both made the Hall of Fame and I didn't. I wasn't a bad influence on them, they were a bad influence on me."

The day Billy got traded was one of the blackest days of my career. Up to that time, Billy was the only roommate I ever had on the road. I have three brothers and they aren't any closer to me than Billy and Whitey were. When they traded Billy, they broke us up, and it broke our hearts.

That night, the three of us went out for one final blast together as Yankees. We drank an ocean of booze and by the end of the night we were all crying. They had broken up our trio and we felt horrible. Nobody felt worse than Billy. He loved the Yankees more than anybody I've ever known. Right up until the day he died in that tragic automobile accident on Christmas night 1989, the only thing he ever really wanted was to be a Yankee.

Billy was going to be in the uniform of the Kansas City Athletics the next day playing against us. That was going to be strange. As luck would have it, Whitey was scheduled to pitch for us. He told Billy that, as sort of a going-away present, he was going to serve one up for him.

"If we're far enough ahead in the game," Whitey said, "I'm going to give you a pitch to hit. If I stand up straight, it's a fastball. If I bend over, it's a curveball. But I'll only do it if we have a safe lead and don't hit a home run off me."

Billy said O.K. and we get a lead and Whitey does like he promised. He stands straight up, throws Billy a fastball, and Billy hits it on a line into the left-field corner. Wouldn't you know it, the ball goes out of the park for a home run. And Billy is laughing all the way around the bases. Whitey was pissed.

In the dugout after the inning, Stengel asked Whitey if he let Billy hit that pitch.

"Oh no, Case," Whitey said with a straight face. "I would never do that."

The next time Billy came to bat, Whitey knocked him on his behind.

In mid-May, Whitey was really on a tear. I never saw him pitch better than he was pitching at that time. He had started six games and won them all, all with complete games. Whitey had never won 20 games in a season, but the way he was going it didn't look like there was any way to stop him from winning 20. Or more.

I had found my stroke again. Two homers in Chicago, another, my sixteenth, in Kansas City. My average was over .400. And we were winning again. It was in Kansas City that we ran into a little trouble.

We were beating the Athletics easily, blowing them out, then late in the game they brought in Tommy Lasorda to pitch against us. The way Tommy tells the story, Lou Boudreau, the Kansas City manager, was burning up at the way we were teeing off on his pitchers.

"Doesn't anyone have the guts to knock these guys down?" Boudreau said.

"I will," Lasorda said, so Boudreau put him in the game.

So Lasorda comes in and he knocks down our eighth-place hitter, then strikes him out. He knocks down Tom Sturdivant and strikes him out. Then he knocks down Bauer and Billy and strikes them out.

Now it's my turn to hit and I'm in the batter's box and I hear Hank and Billy, on the top step of the dugout, yelling at Lasorda. And Tommy didn't back down. He's motioning to the mound and he's yelling back at Hank and Billy, "Here I am, come on out and get me."

Well, you didn't have to ask Billy or Hank twice, and the next thing you know, there was Billy and Lasorda rolling around on the ground and going at it pretty good.

Both benches and both bullpens cleared and there was a good old-fashioned free-for-all that lasted a couple of minutes. Three Kansas City players had to grab Hank, and Billy had Lasorda in a stranglehold in the dirt on the mound.

The umpires pulled them apart and broke up the fight, and after the fracas I put my arm around Lasorda.

"Hey, Tommy," I said. "Hank and Billy are

good guys. They've both been in a slump and they're just a little frustrated. Forget about it."

Years later, Tommy told me he said to himself, "Hey, this Mantle is a nice guy."

I came to bat when play resumed and Lasorda threw me a curveball and I hit it against the wall in left center for a double. I was standing on second base and Lasorda looked at me and started yelling, "You S.O.B., you set me up." I couldn't help laughing.

Isn't it strange that Martin and Lasorda would be rolling on the ground in Kansas City and twenty-one years later they would be opposing managers in the World Series, and two of the best managers in the game, Billy for the Yankees, Lasorda for the Los Angeles Dodgers. Lasorda and Billy got to be pretty good friends in later years. I never got to know Lasorda very well, although I have appeared at a few banquets with him in recent years. I think he's a very good manager and a great storyteller. He's a good motivator, but I don't go for all that hugging stuff and that bleeding Dodger blue. I don't resent Lasorda. I like him. I'm amused by him. But he's a big bullshitter. That's all right. He knows it, and if it works for him, more power to him and I can't knock it.

Lasorda is always talking about "the big

Dodger in the sky," and Billy used to tell him that when Tommy died and went to heaven, he was in for a big surprise. He was going to find out that God is a Yankee fan.

The fight in Kansas City must have got us going, because we won six straight games and got back into first place. Then we ran into that old Yankee killer, Frank Lary, in Detroit. Lary beat us again, a heartbreaker, 3–2. We were leading, 2–1, in the ninth with Whitey pitching, looking for his seventh straight complete-game victory. Money in the bank as far as I was concerned. But Red Wilson rocked Whitey for a two-run homer to win the game, 3–2. Not only did Wilson's homer beat us and end our six-game winning streak, it ended Whitey's six-game winning streak and handed him his first loss of the season. And Lary stopped my hitting streak at nine games.

That may not sound like much of a streak, particularly when you compare it with Joe DiMaggio's record of hitting in 56 consecutive games. That's a record I think never will be broken. Pete Rose took a shot at it about ten years ago and he still fell twelve games short. Hitting in 56 consecutive games is something I cannot even imagine. A nine-game hitting streak was good for me because I struck out and walked so much. In eighteen years, I had 1,734 walks and 1,710 strikeouts. That's 3,444 plate appearances without hitting the ball. Figuring on an average of about 550 plate appearances a season, in a sense I went seven years in the major leagues without ever touching the ball.

After Lary stopped my hitting streak, I got hot again. I had five hits in one game against the Tigers, including my seventeenth home run. I was twelve games ahead of Ruth's pace and I was batting .421. Then I had two more hits and three RBIs when we beat Baltimore, 10–2. But I wasn't the big hitter in that game. Our big hitters were Billy, who had four hits, and Bob Cerv, who hit a grand slam. Cerv was a former football player from Nebraska who would get to be one of my good friends.

In 1961, when Roger Maris and I were battling for the home-run lead, there was a lot of talk that we were envious of one another. Nothing could be further from the truth. Roger and I were very close. Roger, Cerv and I lived together in an apartment in Queens that season. I always liked Roger and respected him as an all-around ballplayer, not just a home-run hitter. He could hit, he could run, he could field and he could throw. He was one of the smartest players I've ever seen. He had great instincts for the game. I never saw him throw to the wrong base or miss the cutoff man, and I never saw him thrown out taking an extra base.

Sure I wanted to break Babe Ruth's record in 1961. Who wouldn't? But if I couldn't do it, I was hoping Roger would. And when I got hurt late in the season and knew I no longer had a shot at the record, I was pulling for Roger to do it as much as anybody, and I was really thrilled for him when he broke the record.

Roger was such a humble man. When he hit a home run, he would run around the bases with his head bowed, like it was no big thing. He almost seemed like he was embarrassed by it. Even when he hit his sixty-first home run off Tracy Stallard in 1961, Roger seemed embarrassed by it. The fans were going crazy, calling for him to come out and take a bow. He didn't want to do it, so the other players had to push him out of the dugout so the fans could give him a standing ovation. The man had just broken the greatest record in sports history, and he had to be forced into taking a curtain call. Can you imagine what a player would do today if he ever hit 62 home runs? There would be curtain calls and high-fives all over the place and the player would probably go right from the field to the front office looking to renegotiate his contract.

No team likes to be shut out and you can bet no team likes to go hitless. We came close in a game against the Red Sox. Willard Nixon held us hitless for seven and two-thirds innings in Boston. Wouldn't you know it would be Billy who would break up the no-hitter with a triple? The Fenway Park crowd booed him for breaking up the no-hitter. Billy loved it. He always believed that being booed on the road was the ultimate tribute to a ballplayer. And it seems that once a pitcher loses a no-hitter late in the game, he's a little shook up and he loses his concentration against the next hitter. I happened to be the next hitter and I followed his triple with my eighteenth homer.

· · ·

On Memorial Day, we had a doubleheader against the Washington Senators in Yankee Stadium. I would be facing Pedro Ramos and Camilo Pascual. They were the Senators' two best pitchers, but I usually hit both of them pretty good. It was Pascual, remember, who was pitching on opening day when I hit those two long home runs in Washington. I can remember Ramos looking at Pascual and laughing, waving a towel and mocking his friend and teammate as if to say, "He wouldn't do that against me."

Ramos was a character. He wound up coming over to the Yankees a few years later and we became teammates and pretty good friends. But now he was one of the Senators' aces. He always used to brag that he could run faster than me. He kept challenging me to a race until Casey said, "All right, you put up $10,000 and we'll put up $10,000 and Mickey will race you, winner take all." But Ramos never did come up with the money. And he never bragged about beating me in a footrace again.

Ramos was funny. The last time we played in Washington, one of our pitchers hit one of their guys and I was leading off the next inning. Ramos was pitching and everybody in the ballpark, except me, knew Ramos was going to hit me to even things up. The first pitch—*whack*—right in the middle of my back. That was the normal thing for a pitcher to do. It was the way we played the game in those days.

The next day, Ramos came over to me at the batting cage during batting practice and said, "Mee-kee, I no want to heet you. They make me do it." I said, "That's all right, Pete, you got to do what they tell you. But the next time you hit me, I'm going to drag a bunt down the first-base line and run right over your ass."

Now it's the first game of the Memorial Day doubleheader. The fifth inning. A 2-2 count and I hit the best ball I ever hit left-handed. It was a high drive that came eighteen inches away from going out of the Stadium. Nobody ever hit a fair ball out of Yankee Stadium and the reporters made a big deal of the shot I hit off Ramos. Some years later, I would hit one off Bill Fischer of Kansas City that came within inches of going out of the Stadium, but this one off Ramos was the closest up to that time. The roof was 117 feet high before it was reconstructed and the ball was hit above the 370-foot sign. They estimated it would have traveled somewhere between 550 and 600 feet if it hadn't hit the roof.

As I rounded third base, I happened to look into the Washington dugout out of the corner of my eye, and there was Camilo Pascual waving a towel at Ramos, just as Ramos had done to him on opening day.

The next day, Ramos came over to me and said, "Mee-kee, I would rather have you run over my ass than to have you heet a ball like that off me."

Pascual pitched the second game and I hit one off him too. Again, it came in the fifth inning. This one went halfway up the upper deck in right field.

We swept the doubleheader from the Senators, 4–3 and 12–5, to open a six-game lead over the White Sox and Indians, who were in a virtual tie for second, with the White Sox ahead by percentage points. The teams behind us were bunched up. The Red Sox were seven and one half games out, the Orioles only eight games behind and the Tigers nine.

Everything was going so good for the team, and me. In forty-one games, I had scored 45 runs, had 65 hits, 135 total bases, 20 homers, 50 RBIs and I was batting .425. For the first time I was beginning to do the things that Casey predicted for me when I came up in 1951.

5

June
Swoon

$\mathcal{B}$aseball can be a frustrating game. For one thing, it's played almost every day, day in and day out, from spring through fall. It's played in all kinds of weather, all sorts of conditions. You have to play it when you're tired, when you're hot, when you're cold, when you may be hurting. There are going to be days when you don't feel like getting out of bed, but you have to play. People pay good money to see you perform, so you have a duty to drag yourself out there if at all possible. And to try to do your best.

It's been said time and time again that baseball is a game in which the best players fail seven out of ten times. If you get three hits in ten at bats—in other words, fail seven out of ten times —you're a .300 hitter and, in today's market, that would bring you millions of dollars. A pitcher who wins 20 games and loses 10 is failing one out of three times, but he's considered extremely successful, a million-dollar property and a potential Hall of Famer.

Consistency is the sign of greatness. Hit .300 over a span of ten years—in other words, fail 70 percent of the time for ten years—and you'll probably earn millions of dollars and make the Hall of Fame.

The same thing applies to teams. A team that wins 95 games is going to win a championship more often than not. That means you can lose 67 games, about 43 percent of the games you play, and still win a championship.

So it stands to reason that even the best of teams, the championship teams, the great teams, are going to have a slump at least once during a season of 162 games (154 in 1956). Maybe more than once. Every team, even the best of them, is going to hit a dry spell. In 1956, ours came in June.

We lost the first four games we played in the

month. In the first one, we were beaten for the third time by Frank Lary, which was getting to be a habit and very frustrating. Then after a rainout, we played the Tigers a doubleheader and lost both games, which figured. Give this bunch of guys a day (and night) off and they were going to be in no shape to play ball the next day. Then Kansas City came to town and we lost again.

We played sloppy baseball in the first game of a three-game series against Kansas City. We made five errors and Billy made three of them. I decided it was best not to say anything to him about it. Billy never was what you would call a good loser, which, I suppose, is one reason he always was a winner. I hit my twenty-first homer of the season, my first since Memorial Day, but we couldn't overcome the five errors.

Casey was getting a little irritable. He accused us of being complacent, but other than that he didn't say too much. I found that Casey's philosophy of managing was to lay off when the team was in a slump, but drive us hard when we were winning.

Casey was special as a manager. They claimed he was a push-button manager, but that was silly. Obviously, if you don't have the players, you can't win. Casey didn't win with Boston and Brooklyn, but he was the same manager.

The only thing a manager can do is keep the guys who were not playing wanting to play, and Stengel was a master at that. Guys lose interest sitting on the bench and Casey had by far the best bench I've ever seen. There were guys sitting on that bench that were as good as the guys playing and it was Casey's job to keep them all involved.

Another thing a manager has to do is control the team and take charge, and there never was any doubt that Casey was in charge. He was also a great psychologist. He knew when to get on you and when to lay off.

Casey got a lot of credit for platooning, but when you have the players, like Gene Woodling and Hank Bauer in right field, it's easy to platoon. Whoever he put out there would do the job.

But you can't take anything away from Stengel. He had the players, sure, but he knew how to use them. I liked playing for him. He was like a second father to me. My dad died in the spring of 1952, and I always felt Casey kind of took his place.

Whatever Stengel did, you have to say it worked, judging from his record of five straight world championships and ten pennants and seven world championships in twelve seasons.

After losing three games to Detroit and the

first game to Kansas City, we beat the Athletics the last two games of the three-game series to take the pressure off. We needed those wins because the Cleveland Indians were coming to town for a three-game weekend series and they had shaved our lead down to just four and a half games, with the White Sox just a game behind the Indians.

In 1954, when we won 103 games and still lost the pennant by eight games because Cleveland won 111, the Indians had the best pitching staff I ever faced. They had two 23-game winners (Bob Lemon and Early Wynn), a 19-game winner (Mike Garcia) and a 15-game winner (Art Houtteman). They also had Bob Feller, who was thirty-five years old but still threw as hard as anybody around, Hal Newhouser, a veteran who had been a Most Valuable Player in the American League twice, and a great lefty-righty bullpen combination of Don Mossi (the lefty) and Ray Narleski.

Now, two years later, Lemon, Wynn and Garcia were still around, pitching as well as ever. Narleski was still there. And they had come up with a hard-throwing left-hander named Herb Score. That's why I knew we could never feel we were a cinch to win the pennant, no matter how big a lead we had.

In the first game of the series, Wynn stuck the bats up our ass and beat us, 9–0. And in the second game of the series, we blew a 6–0 lead and got beat, 15–8. All of a sudden, our lead was two and a half games. My average had slipped under .400 and I had hit only one home run since Memorial Day. We were in trouble.

We needed a stopper and Johnny Kucks came through, as he did for us all season. Kucks was a tall, skinny right-hander from New Jersey who grew up a Yankee fan. He was a sinkerball pitcher, which meant he kept the ball on the ground and gave up very few home runs. So he could give up a lot of hits and not get hurt. Going for a sweep of the three-game series that would have cut our lead to a game and a half, the Indians got nine hits off Kucks. But he was tough in the clutch and we beat them, 6–0. That upped our lead to three and a half games and took the pressure off.

The big hit in the game was Joe Collins' three-run pinch-hit homer off Bob Lemon. Collins was a tough coal miner from Scranton, Pennsylvania, and one of the best clutch hitters I ever saw. He was another of those guys that Casey platooned who probably could have been a regular with any other team. He was coming to the end of his career, but he still could deliver a big hit in the clutch.

I remember one time Joe was hitting in front of me and he hit a long home run to right field. When he came around the bases, I was waiting to shake his hand and he just looked at me and said, "Chase that one, big boy."

Now it's my turn to bat and I hit one about fifteen feet deeper than Collins' and I round the bases and come into the dugout and I just looked at Joe with a smile on my face. And Joe just said, "Go shit in your hat," and walked away.

The schedule had us off after the Indian series, but we couldn't even enjoy the day off. The club had arranged for the whole team to go to the theater at night to see the play *Damn Yankees*, which struck me as a silly idea. We were to meet at Yankee Stadium and go together by bus to the theater. Some guys didn't show up and I wish I hadn't either.

I never was much for plays. They just didn't interest me. I preferred to go to the movies. I liked Westerns. John Wayne and that kind of stuff. In fact, *Damn Yankees* is the only play I ever saw.

It was about an old guy in Washington who's this real big Senator fan and he's frustrated because his favorite team keeps finishing in the second division every year. He meets a guy who turns out to be the devil and this old guy, the Washington fan, makes a deal with the devil. If the old guy promises to give the devil his soul, the devil will turn him into this young stud baseball player who hits tremendous home runs.

So the guy becomes young again, he changes his name to Joe Hardy and he joins the Senators and helps them beat the Yankees. People said the author patterned this Joe Hardy after me. I don't know if that's true. Another thing I didn't know was why the club would want us to see a play where the Yankees lose the pennant. I didn't like the idea of watching us lose and I know Billy wasn't too happy about it either. Both of us could hardly wait for the show to end so we could get the hell out of there and hit our regular spots . . . Toots's, Danny's Hideaway.

We were in the middle of a slump, but we had to go to Newark one afternoon because the club had scheduled a parade in the city that for many years had the Yankees' top farm team in the International League. We're trying to win a pennant and we had to go to plays and parades. No wonder we were losing.

That was going to be some parade if we kept losing and fell out of first place. Fortunately, just about that time we got hot again. We won four straight and I hit home runs in three straight games to give me 24 on June 16.

We opened a three-game series in Detroit, which was my favorite park to hit in. It has a great hitting background, so you can see the ball coming out of the pitcher's hand, the power alleys are reachable and the balls seem to carry well in that ballpark.

The worst park for me to hit in was Yankee Stadium. I didn't pull the ball like Yogi did or Roger Maris did. All my power was to right center and left center and it was 457 feet to left center, 461 to straightaway center and 407 to right center.

I once heard an interview with Ted Williams in which he was asked if he'd rather play in Yankee Stadium than Fenway Park. And Ted said he'd rather hit in Fenway because they would pitch to him there. When he came to the Stadium, they wouldn't even pitch to him. Although it never mattered to Ted because when he hit it right, it went out of any ballpark.

Since they remodeled the Stadium, it's 411 to left center and 385 to right center and guys are pissed off because it's too far. How about Jose Canseco? He thinks they should move the fences in in Oakland. He wants to play in a Little League park. Let him play in a Little League park, then he can make $10 million. It makes me laugh. These guys today should have seen Yankee Stadium before they renovated it. Then what would they say?

The fences weren't close in Detroit, but they were fair, and because of the hitting background and the balls carrying so well, I always hit well there. In my career, I hit four balls over the roof in Detroit and I believe I'm the only player, home or visiting, to do that.

Ted Williams hit three over the roof and Norm Cash hit three and Norm always used to get on me because he was only one behind me.

"Hell," I told him, "you play half your games there, seventy-seven games a year. I play eleven. You oughta hit more over the roof than I do."

I also hit three balls into the upper deck in center field in Detroit in a doubleheader, two right-handed and one left-handed, and I know nobody else ever did that.

Going to Detroit also meant a chance to visit with Mel Ott, who was a Tiger broadcaster at the time.

Ott had been one of the greatest stars in New York history. He came out of Louisiana and joined the New York Giants in 1926 without ever playing a day in the minor leagues. He was just seventeen years old at the time, and he spent his entire career with the Giants, all twenty-two years, something that's almost unheard of nowadays. He even managed the Giants at the end of his career for seven seasons, six of them as a player-manager. Also unheard of today.

Ott was an amazing guy. He stood only five-nine and weighed about 170 in his prime, but he was strong. He hit 511 home runs in his career and held the National League record for career home runs for many years, until guys like Hank Aaron, Willie Mays, Willie McCovey, Eddie Mathews, Ernie Banks and Mike Schmidt came along and passed him.

In my restaurant, we have paintings of every guy who ever hit 500 home runs in his career, fourteen of them. People will come in and they'll quickly identify thirteen of them, but the one guy they have trouble with is Ott, probably because he played so long ago. When he played, there was no television, so people never got a good look at him. I'll bet he could have walked into any place in New York in his prime and very few people would have recognized him. But that doesn't take away from the great record he made.

Some people put down Ott's home-run total because he played in the Polo Grounds, which had a very unusual shape for a ballpark. I played there in the 1951 World Series and it was weird. The right-field line was 267 feet and the left-field line 287. But it pulled away toward center field, where it was about 500 feet to straightaway center. It was easy to hit the ball out of the park, but you had to be a dead pull hitter, which Ott was. I never saw him play in person, but I've seen him on film. He would lift his right leg high in the air before he hit, which is very unorthodox. Somehow, he managed to get the leg down in time to plant it and drive the ball to right.

I don't care if it was a short pop to right in the Polo Grounds; 511 is a lot of home runs, even if you're hitting in a telephone booth.

· · ·

Strangely enough, I hit more home runs while batting
left-handed than right-handed.

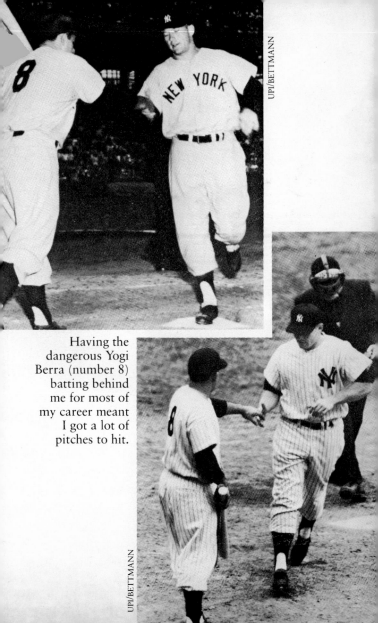

Having the dangerous Yogi Berra (number 8) batting behind me for most of my career meant I got a lot of pitches to hit.

UPI/BETTMANN

UPI/BETTMANN

In 1964 Yogi was
my manager. He
won a pennant, lost
the World Series to
the Cardinals in
seven games . . . and
was fired. And
George Steinbrenner
wasn't even the
owner.

The Three Musketeers . . . Whitey, me and Billy. We cried—
and drank—the night Billy was traded to Kansas City.

The 1956 New York Yankees. Not the best team I ever played
on (I still pick 1961), but not too bad.

Almost picked off in Washington. I must have spotted something nice in the stands and lost my concentration.

I hit my twenty-fifth home run and we beat the Tigers, 7–4, for our fifth straight. My home run came batting left-handed against a right-hander named Paul Foytack, and was one of the hardest balls I hit all year. What was funny about it was that the wind was blowing straight in all day and in batting practice everybody was saying, "Nobody will hit one out today." But I hit one over the roof.

The roof is 110 feet high and the ball sailed over the roof just to the right of the 370-foot sign and landed on Trumbull Avenue. I heard later that a man driving in his car near the ballpark heard Mel Ott describe the ball going out of the park and saw it land in the street. He stopped his car and got out and retrieved the ball. The next day he brought it to the park and I signed it for him.

We swept the three-game series in Detroit to give us a seven-game winning streak and increase our lead to five and a half games. Johnny Kucks won his ninth game against the Tigers and Whitey came in for one of his rare relief appearances to save it for Kucks. And to show how much I liked hitting in Detroit, I hit three home runs in the three games, giving me 27 for the season and putting me eighteen games ahead of Babe Ruth. The papers were beginning to print the number of games I was ahead of the Babe, and the writers were beginning to ask me about breaking the record. But I just told them it was too early to think of that, and it was.

Two of the homers came in the final game of the series. A funny thing happened during the game. A fan jumped over the low fence in left field and came running onto the field. Let me just say that it's not a good idea for fans to do that. For one thing, it breaks a player's concentration. For another, as a player, you never know what that fan is going to do. He could be some crazy with a knife or a gun. You never kr

Yogi was playing left field for us day and the fan runs up and shakes his han . Then the fan looks up and sees me and he starts coming over to center field. But he never did let loose of Yogi. The fan is running toward me and he's still holding Yogi's hand, dragging him with him. Yogi's got his glove off and he's trying to get loose from the guy, who has dragged him halfway to center field. The security guards came and took the guy away.

Although I led the league with 27 homers in mid-June, I still hadn't been able to cut down on my strikeouts. With my 27 homers, I also had 32 strikeouts. Of those 32 strikeouts, 10 of them were looking and Casey was always yelling at the umpires about that. There were three umpires I thought were not giving me a fair shake. Ed Runge, Ed Hurley and Bill Valentine. All a pitcher had to do was throw one close and they'd call it a strike. I don't know why. I never did argue with umpires too much, but after I retired and I was talking with some umpires, they told me, "You never did yell at us, but we couldn't stand the way you looked at us."

I had this habit of looking at them with disgust. I'd turn around and stare at them like they were nuts, and even though I didn't say anything, they thought it looked like I was trying to show them up.

Casey used to get on the umpires all the time. He never got on me for striking out. In fact, he tried to get me not to blow my top when I struck out. Me and Billy. When I would strike out, I'd kick the water cooler or punch it, I was so pissed off. Billy would throw his bat or his helmet. One day, Casey decided to talk to us about it.

"Look," Casey said. "Strikeouts are part of the game. You're going to strike out. That's O.K. I don't want you to throw things or punch things. You might get hurt, or you might hurt one of your teammates. Just laugh it off."

Well, that gave Billy an idea.

"Hey, Mick," he said. "Let's try it. The next time you strike out, just laugh it off. And I'll do the same thing."

So we did it. I'd strike out and I'd go back to the bench laughing.

"Imagine that, ha, ha, ha," I'd say. "I struck out again."

And Billy would strike out and gently put his bat and his helmet on the ground and he'd say, "Ha, ha, ha, how about that guy striking me out on a hanging curveball? Ha, ha, ha."

This went on for a couple of days and we could see that Stengel was getting pissed.

Finally, one day Billy strikes out and he comes back and he's laughing, and the Old Man just looks at him and says, "All right, that will be enough of that shit."

Baseball is a game of streaks. After winning seven straight, we turned right around and lost four straight, two of them to the Indians, and suddenly our lead was down to one game, because all through our streak Cleveland had been hot too. We left Cleveland and went to Kansas City and I got my first look at the "Mantle Shift."

Lou Boudreau, who invented the "Williams Shift" against Ted Williams when he managed the Indians, was now the manager of Kansas City. And he was the first one to use the shift against me. He did it when I was batting left-handed. He put three infielders on the right side and left only the third baseman between second and third.

Boudreau did it to me for a different reason than he did it against Williams. He knew Williams never would try to hit the ball to the opposite field. That was Williams' only weakness as a hitter. He was too stubborn, or too proud, or both, to take advantage of the shift. He figured he could still pull the ball and either hit it out of the park or hit it through the infield no matter how many guys they put over there. Usually Williams hit the ball hard and if it wasn't hit straight at a fielder, the defense would have no chance.

With me, it was different. Boudreau wanted me to bunt. What he didn't know was that I couldn't bunt the ball to third base batting left-handed. The only bunt I could execute batting left-handed was a drag bunt down the first-base line or between the pitcher and the first baseman.

But when I first saw the shift, I would try to bunt the ball down the third-base line or try to hit a ground ball through the left side. But Casey told me, "Hey, the hell with that. Don't be trying to hit ground balls. That's the reason he's doing that. He wants you to bunt or hit ground balls. He wants you to hit singles. We want you to hit home runs."

Another time we were playing Kansas City and there were two out in the ninth inning and we were trailing by one run. I came to bat against Satchel Paige, who had been a great star in the old Negro leagues but was now about fifty years old and finally getting his chance to play in the major leagues. I tried to bunt to get on base and I got thrown out and we lost the game.

After the game, the reporters asked Paige, "What did you think of Mantle trying to bunt for a base hit with two out in the ninth?"

And old Satch said, "Shoot, if he'da told me, I'da give him first base."

6

Stars in My Eyes

The early part of July provided one of those good news/bad news situations. The good news was a two-home-run game. It was against Washington, as you may have guessed, and that gave me 29 for the season and put me eight games ahead of Babe Ruth's pace. The home runs, on the first day of the month, were hit from each side of the plate. It was the second time in my career I had done that. I would end up doing it ten times in my career, a record I'm very proud of.

The two home runs also gave me 100 hits, a good start toward my first 200-hit season. As it turned out, I would end up with only 188, and I never would get 200 hits in a season in my career. That's one thing I would have liked to do. Part of the reason I never did was that I got so many walks (more than 100 ten times) and I was injured so much. The most at bats I ever had in a season was 549 in 1952, my second year with the Yankees. In eighteen seasons, I had more than 500 official at bats only eight times.

When Dave Winfield was traded by the Yankees to the California Angels, I read an article that pointed out that in his nine seasons with the Yankees, Winfield had six seasons in which he drove in at least 100 runs, and I had only four 100-RBI seasons in my eighteen years.

I'm not taking anything away from Winfield, who is a good ballplayer and a guy I thought played hard all the time. But if you look at his record, you'll notice that six times in his nine years with the Yankees, Winfield had more than 550 official at bats, and once he batted more than 600 times. I never came to bat more than 550 times in my entire career. In 1956, my Triple Crown year, for example, I came to bat only 533 times.

Winfield never walked 100 times in a season.

His highest total with the Yankees was 77. Usually, he was in the fifties and sixties. I walked 100 or more times in a season ten times in my career, including one stretch of 100 or more walks in eight out of nine years. Once I walked 99 times, another season I walked 94 times. Another thing. When I was playing, the schedule was 154 games for most of my career. Now they play 162 games, eight more games, a potential of about thirty more at bats. It makes a big difference.

Take Pete Rose, for example. He had 200 or more hits ten times in his career. But don't forget, he was a leadoff hitter, he was pretty much injury-free throughout his career and he never was a home-run threat, so he didn't walk a lot.

I once looked up Rose's record and in twenty-four seasons he walked more than 100 times just once. Usually, he'd walk about 60 times. Seventeen times he had more than 600 official at bats in a season. I'm not putting Pete down, because he was a terrific player and got all those hits, but give me 600 at bats and I know I would have had 200 hits. Hell, I would have had 50 base hits on bunts.

It's like the comment I made about Jose Canseco that got so much attention. He had just become the first player in baseball history to hit 40 homers and steal 40 bases in one season, and I said, "If I'da known it was such a big deal, I'da done it myself a few times." I probably would have too. But we didn't steal that much in those days. The most steals I ever had in one season was 21. Not that I couldn't have stolen more. I could have. It just wasn't that important back then, especially with a team like ours that hit the ball out of the ballpark. And with my bad legs, Stengel didn't want me to steal anyway.

Today, players seem to steal just for the sake of stealing, to pad their stats. In my day, we stole to win a ball game.

But anyway, back to early July. The bad news was another injury. After seeing our lead dwindle to just one game on June 24, we put on a little spurt to open up some ground. On the morning of July 4, it was still a race, with two teams on our tail. We led the White Sox by three and a half games, the Indians by four and a half. The Red Sox had slipped nine and a half games behind.

Boston came into Yankee Stadium for a doubleheader on the Fourth of July. We went into the ninth inning of the first game with the score tied, 6–6. The Red Sox had a runner on second, the go-ahead run, and somebody hit a single to center. I had a shot at cutting the guy down at home and I tried to put too much on the throw. As a result, I felt a twinge in my right knee.

We lost the first game, 7–6, and as it turned out I had strained the lateral ligaments in the knee. I sat out the second game of the doubleheader, which we won, and three more games, which we also won, proving that we had such talent and depth, they didn't need me to win. That's what made this team, and most of the Yankee teams I played on, so great. We always had such depth and a lot of guys who were part-time players who could have been regulars with most other teams.

The team didn't miss me and we came up to the All-Star break in great shape. Our trainer, Gus Mauch, used to say, "Get twenty games over .500, then go on a long winning streak." We had won five straight games to put us twenty-six games over .500 at the break, at 52–26, and we led the league by six and a half games over the White Sox, who slipped ahead of the Indians. In the first half of the season, the battle for second was closer than the battle for first. The White Sox and Indians kept taking turns in second.

I came up to the All-Star break with 29 home runs, one game ahead of Babe Ruth's pace, and I was batting .371. And we had two pitchers, Johnny Kucks and Whitey Ford, whose combined record was 21–8; Kucks was 11–4, Whitey 10–4.

One thing I have always regretted about my career is that I never took the All-Star Game seriously enough. I usually looked at it as a few days off to more or less rest and to party. I liked to get together with other guys in baseball that I didn't normally see, like Don Drysdale, Eddie Mathews and Harvey Kuenn, and hoist a few.

If I had it to do all over, I'd take a greater interest in the All-Star Game, because the National League beat us so often. I never realized it meant so much.

I can remember guys like Mays and Aaron and Banks playing hard, taking it seriously. Even if they got taken out of the game, they were over there, still on the bench rooting for their team. As soon as I got out of the game, I'd go in, take a shower and get a beer.

In 1967, the All-Star Game was played in Anaheim. It was my next-to-last year and I wasn't having a very good season. I didn't deserve to make the All-Star team and I really didn't want to go. I wanted to go home to Dallas and play golf and take a few days off. But they put me on the team anyway and I had no choice.

That's another thing that's changed. Today, players look for an excuse to duck out on the All-Star Game, unless they have a clause in their contracts that gives them a bonus for making the All-Star team. Then, it's a different story. In my day, players had no such bonuses and they felt they had an obligation to their teams and to the game of baseball to play in the game if they were chosen. Believe me, there were many times when I was hurting when I would have preferred to take the three days off and rest. But I played anyway.

But in 1967 I went home at the break and I was in Dallas the morning of the game playing golf at Preston Trails Country Club. Preston Trails is this exclusive club twenty miles outside of Dallas. It has only 250 members. There never will be any more than 250 members and it's all men, no women. They had a sign up, FOR MEN ONLY, and one of those women's lib groups protested, so they had to change the sign to read: A MEN'S CLUB. They couldn't advertise men only because that would be discrimination. I told them they should allow one woman in, but they didn't go for my suggestion.

I was one of the first members of the club, and when I joined in 1965, the membership fee was $6,000. But I felt out of place. They had members like the Hunts and the Murchisons, some of the wealthiest men in Texas, and I figured, "What am I doing in that group?" I didn't know anybody and I felt I didn't belong with those people. I paid my first $3,000 and I was considering not paying the other $3,000 because I didn't feel comfortable there at the time. But Ed Haggar, who owns the Haggar Company, talked me into paying the other $3,000.

"Mick," Ed said, "you gotta go ahead and pay the other $3,000. The membership is worth $25,000 already."

So I paid the other $3,000 and I'm glad I did. Now a membership is worth $75,000.

Anyway, I was at Preston Trails playing golf the morning of the 1967 All-Star Game and it was arranged for me to fly to the game. So I left the golf course and went to Dallas International Airport and flew to Los Angeles. In Los Angeles, they picked me up in a helicopter and flew me to Anaheim, where I had a police escort to the ballpark. I got to the park just as the game was starting. I didn't even make the team picture.

Baltimore had won the American League pennant the year before, so my buddy Hank

Bauer, who had managed the Orioles, was managing the American League All-Star team. I get to the ballpark and into uniform and walk into the dugout and I say to the players, "Hi, guys, how you doing?"

Hank comes over and says, "You want to hit?"

"Sure," I said.

"O.K.," Hank said. "You hit for Chance [American League pitcher Dean Chance] in the third inning."

That was the game in which thirty batters struck out on both teams. So I put on a helmet and went up to hit against Juan Marichal and I struck out. I said goodbye to everybody and went back into the clubhouse, took off my uniform, got into my clothes, took the police car back to Anaheim airport, got in a helicopter and flew to Los Angeles and took a plane back home to Dallas. When I got to Dallas, I went back to Preston Trails. I had a two-hour time difference in my favor and that was the game that went fifteen innings. By the time I got back to Preston Trails, the game was still on. So as I was sitting in the clubhouse at Preston Trails watching the end of the game, some of the guys who saw me there said, "Damn, didn't we just see you strike out?"

. . .

The 1956 All-Star Game happened to be in Washington, one of my favorite parks to hit in and the place where we'd just finished playing. That meant I didn't have to travel to get to the game. More time for partying.

One thing I did like about the All-Star Game was getting to be a teammate of my idol, Ted Williams, even if it was just for a day. It was a thrill for me just to be on the same team with him, just as it was a thrill to be on the same team with Joe DiMaggio. They are the two greatest players I ever saw; Williams the greatest hitter, Joe the greatest all-around player.

Williams was one guy on the American League team who took the All-Star Game seriously. Not only was he such a great competitor, he was a very proud man and this was his chance to show his greatness in front of players from the other league, the press from all over the country and a national audience.

I used to love to talk to Williams about hitting—or, rather, listen to Williams talk about hitting, because with Ted, you didn't get to do much talking. He did all the talking in that loud, booming voice of his. He loved to talk about hitting. It was his favorite subject, next to fishing, and he made a science out of hitting. He could talk about it for hours—and he usually did. All the technical stuff that I didn't understand.

Ted liked to talk to other hitters and ask them their theories, things that he might be able to apply and use himself. He was always asking questions, looking for new theories on hitting, telling his own theories, anything to learn more about hitting and maybe improve. One time, he started asking me which was my power hand, which hand did I use to guide the bat. And when I left him, I started thinking about all the things he told me and I didn't get a hit for about twenty-five times at bat.

Hell, I just used to go up there swinging. About the only thing I understood about hitting is that you stood up there, looked for the ball and hit it as hard as you could. One time, I struck out four times and I came back to the bench and sat down next to Whitey and I said, "Slick, what the hell am I doing wrong?"

He said, "I think you're shutting your eyes before you lunge."

Thanks, pal. Big help you are.

I listened to Williams and I watched him hit in the batting cage and it was like a clinic.

Casey managed the American League and he batted me fourth, behind Williams, so I had the best seat in the house, in the on-deck circle, when the greatest hitter in the history of the game was at bat.

We went into the sixth inning with the National League beating us again, 5–0. Nellie Fox was batting second and he started us off with a single. There was a guy I really respected. A tough little guy. Good competitor. Always had that big chew of tobacco in his mouth that made the cheek bulge out. He played just about every game and he was a great hitter. Not for power, but he had over 2,600 hits and a lifetime batting average of .288. Good for a second baseman.

So Fox starts us off with a single and Williams is up against Warren Spahn and he hits a home run. Now it was 5–2 and it was my turn to hit. I never did hit Spahn very good. I hit against him in a couple of World Series and All-Star Games and he never seemed to try to work on me, just threw me high fastballs all the time. I think I kept looking for something like his screwball, and he would just throw me high fastballs and he'd get me. This time, I got him. He threw me a high fastball and I hit it out of the park, back-to-back home runs for Williams and me. That made it 5–3, but that's all we got. The National League beat us again, 7–3.

We had gone into the All-Star break with a five-game winning streak and we picked right up where we left off. We made it six in a row. Then seven. Then eight. We had a nine-and-a-half-game lead with the second-place White Sox coming into Yankee Stadium for a three-game series. It was a chance to put them away.

We swept the White Sox a doubleheader to increase our winning streak to ten straight. The third game of the series was rained out, but we made it eleven straight by beating the Tigers, a 4–0 shutout for Johnny Kucks, who raised his record to 14–4. We led the league by ten and a half games.

On July 20, we beat Kansas City, 6–2, to open an eleven-game lead, our biggest of the season. Whitey won to make his record 12–4 and he also tied an American League record when he struck out six straight batters.

Whitey never was known as a power pitcher, so the strikeout streak surprised a few people. Not me. Nothing Whitey did surprised me. I kidded him, accused him of cheating. But Whitey said he didn't start cheating until much later, at the end of his career, when he no longer had his best stuff and he felt he had to do something to compensate in order to survive. Like I said. Nothing Whitey did ever surprised me. That's why I started calling him "Slick." Later, he started calling me "Slick" too.

One year, after the 1961 season, we had made a commitment to play in the first baseball players' golf tournament in Palm Springs, a charity event with the proceeds going to help old ballplayers in need. We took Merlyn and Joan with us and we stayed with an old friend, Cecil Simmons, who was a casino boss at the Desert Inn in Las Vegas.

After the tournament, Cecil invited us to be his guest in Las Vegas. Our wives were excited about it, so we went. We flew to Vegas in a private plane, and all the way there, Cecil kept telling us that "Betty" was going to pick us up. It was Betty this and Betty that and we had no idea who Betty was.

We get to Las Vegas and waiting for us at the airport was this beautiful blonde. I recognized her right away. It was Betty Grable. I had been crazy about her since I was ten years old. That was Cecil's friend Betty. She drove us to our hotel. The next day, she and Cecil cooked us a fried chicken dinner. I couldn't wait to see Billy and tell him Betty Grable had cooked fried chicken for me.

At the time, Betty Grable was married to Harry James, the bandleader, and he was a big baseball fan. They lived next door to Cecil and we spent a lot of time with them, mostly talking baseball with Harry. They turned out to be two of the nicest people you'd ever want to meet.

I'm not much of a gambler, but one night we decided to take Merlyn and Joan to the casino. First we stopped at the bar in the casino. Our plan was to feed our wives a couple of drinks, they would get tired and go off to bed, then Whitey and I would gamble a little and have some fun.

Merlyn had about two screwdrivers, then excused herself and went off to bed. But we couldn't get rid of Joan. She stayed with us, drink for drink, and I was getting stiff and so was Whitey, but Joanie was cold sober.

Finally, at about 3 A.M., Joan went to bed and Whitey and I were left to have some fun.

"Let's do a little gambling," I said.

"All right," Whitey said. "Give me $50."

Whitey put fifty of his own with mine and went to the roulette table. Ten minutes later, he had blown the $100.

"Hey, Slick," Whitey said. "Give me another $50."

Again he took my fifty, put it with fifty of his own and went off to the roulette table. Another ten minutes passed, and here was Whitey back. He had blown another $100. Now we were out $200 between us.

"Let me show you how to gamble," I boasted. "Give me another $50, Slick."

I left Whitey at the bar, went to the blackjack table and returned about an hour later and dumped a pile of bills in front of him. It came to about $1,700. Whitey couldn't believe it.

What had happened, I ran into Cecil Simmons at the tables and he decided he would coach me. He'd look at my cards, then he would look at the dealer's hole card and he would tell me to hit or not. It wasn't cheating . . . exactly.

At one point, I had nineteen showing and Cecil told me to take a hit.

"Are you crazy?" I said. "Hit on nineteen?"

"Hit," he said.

You see, Cecil had looked at the dealer's hole card and the dealer had twenty, so I had nothing to lose by hitting on nineteen. So that's how I won the $1,700 and impressed Whitey that a country boy from Oklahoma can be just as slick as a city kid from the sidewalks of New York.

· · ·

Late in the month, we played Kansas City a doubleheader at Yankee Stadium and split it. In the first game, when I came to bat in the sixth inning, Lou Boudreau put that damn shift on again, three men on the right side of the infield, one between second and third. Despite Casey telling me to ignore it and swing normally, I decided to bunt toward third and beat it out for a hit. I guess that showed them. My next time up, in the seventh, there was no shift. I hit my thirty-second home run of the season.

We went back on the road, to Chicago, feeling pretty good about things. We figured we could put the White Sox away, and we did. But the Indians were hanging in. Still, we had an eight-and-a-half-game lead late in July. I figured that was a safe enough lead, so I began to look occasionally at how things were going in the National League, kind of looking ahead to the World Series. The Milwaukee Braves were in first place, six games ahead of the Dodgers. I was hoping the Dodgers could come back and win over there and we could play them in the World Series. I wanted to get them back for what happened in 1955.

• • •

Toward the end of the month, we went to Kansas City, where Casey Stengel was a big favorite. He was born there and lived most of his life there, although he moved to Glendale, California, in his later years. Casey even went to school in Kansas City when he was studying to be a left-handed dentist, before he gave that up and concentrated on baseball. Whenever we went to Kansas City, some old guy would come up to Casey in the lobby of the hotel and call him "Dutch," which was his nickname when he was a boy. Casey would carry on this long conversation with the guy that nobody could understand and when the old guy left and somebody asked Casey who the guy was, Casey would just shrug and say, "Damned if I know."

Other times he might run into a guy he played ball with in the minor leagues, and then he'd tell you, in great detail, everything about the guy, including something that happened in 1917. He was some character. Usually when he talked, you couldn't make out a word he said. But when he had to get a point across, you never missed his message. He was dumb like a fox.

A few years earlier, there was this Senate

committee, headed by Senator Estes Kefauver, that was investigating antitrust practices in the United States. Baseball had been under some criticism for being exempt from antitrust and the committee called a few baseball players and executives to Washington to testify at the hearing.

I was called and so were Ted Williams and Stan Musial and Casey. When it was Casey's turn to testify, he took the stand and Senator Kefauver asked him one question and Casey went into his famous double-talk that they called Stengelese. He went on for about twenty-five minutes, talking about how he broke into baseball in Kankakee, Illinois, in 1909 and then going through his whole career, how he managed in Brooklyn and Boston, then went back to manage in the minor leagues in Oakland before joining the Yankees.

He had the whole place laughing and nobody could understand a word he said. After about twenty-five or thirty minutes, Senator Kefauver must have had enough of that, because he said, "All right, Mr. Stengel, you can step down. Thank you very much."

I think Kefauver would have excused Casey a lot earlier, but the Old Man didn't stop talking long enough for Kefauver to get a word in.

After Casey finished, they called on me. I was nervous. I didn't know what to say. What did I know about antitrust? So Senator Kefauver asked me if I thought baseball was a monopoly.

"I don't know about that, Senator," I said. "But I agree with everything Casey just said."

That broke the place up.

Casey's sixty-sixth birthday was July 30, but we would be out of Kansas City by then, so before the game on July 29, the fans stood up and sang "Happy Birthday" to him. Knowing Casey, I'm sure the best birthday present for him was a 5–3 victory for our fifth straight win and a nine-game lead over Cleveland.

After we left Kansas City, we went into Cleveland for a four-game series with a chance to put the Indians away for good, just as we had done with the White Sox. Whitey pitched the first game against Bob Lemon, who always was tough on us, as he was on everybody. But Lemon didn't have it this day. We scored seven runs in the second inning off him, when I hit a grand slam. I hit another homer to give me 34 for the season and I was keeping pace with Babe Ruth's record, one home run ahead of him after ninety-seven games. I knocked in six runs in our 13–6 win. Whitey won his fourteenth and our lead was up to ten games.

7

I Chase Ruth, Williams Chases Me

The Indians still felt they had a chance to catch us even after we went into Cleveland and bombed Bob Lemon to win the first game of the four-game series, which gave us a ten-game lead. They still felt their pitching staff could bring them back into the race, and in fact they would end up with three 20-game winners, Lemon, Early Wynn and Herb Score. They still had Mike Garcia and they had Don Mossi and Ray Narleski in the bullpen.

Lemon had that great sinker and exceptional

control and he knew how to pitch. He changed speeds and kept you off balance, but he could bust the fastball when he had you set up for it. And like a lot of pitchers of the day, he wasn't afraid to pitch inside.

When it came to pitching inside, Early Wynn was the master. He was the meanest pitcher I ever faced. He hated to have a ball hit hard back at him. I hit a ball back at him once when he was with Washington. It went through the box for a single. When I was on first, he told the Senators' first baseman, Roy Sievers, to get behind me when he was holding me on, instead of in front of me, the way a first baseman is supposed to hold a runner on base. Then he would throw the ball to first, as if he was trying to pick me off, but he was really trying to hit me.

Wynn would just as soon knock you down as look at you. For any reason. If you crowded the plate. If you hit a long foul off him. If you so much as took a good cut against him. *Bam!* He'd knock you down. He used to try to knock down Yogi, but Yogi would pick himself right up out of the dirt and hit a rope somewhere. Yogi just wore Wynn out, and the more he did, the more Wynn would knock him down; and the more Wynn knocked Yogi down, the more Yogi would hit him.

They used to say that Wynn was so mean he'd knock down his own mother. When somebody asked him about that, Wynn just looked at the guy and said, "Mother was a helluva hitter."

Feller was getting old by the time I faced him, only a spot starter, but he was still great. He didn't throw as hard as he once did, but he could still run it up there a few times a game. And he had a great overhand curveball. I've heard it said that Feller threw harder in his prime than any pitcher in the history of baseball, and I believe it. They didn't have guns to measure the speed of a pitch in those days, but people tell me he was consistently in the high nineties.

Feller's record proves his greatness. He won 266 games and lost only 162. He struck out 3,271 batters. Six times he won 20 or more games. Seven times he led the American League in strikeouts. One year he struck out 348 batters. And he pitched three no-hitters. Plus, he missed four of the most productive years of his career when he went into military service in World War II. He had won 24, 27 and 25 games, and struck out 246, 261 and 260 batters when he went into service. Then, when he came out, he won 26 games and struck out 348, so you can just imagine what he might have done in the four years he missed.

Garcia didn't have the best record of the Indians' pitchers. Lemon, Wynn and Feller all made the Hall of Fame, but Garcia didn't. Still, he was the toughest of the Indians' pitchers for me to hit. They called him the "Big Bear" and he was almost as mean on the mound as Wynn. He liked to pitch up and in and he threw a heavy ball. I used to bunt against him a lot.

Herb Score was another one of the best pitchers I ever faced. I thought he had a chance to be as good as Sandy Koufax if he didn't get hurt. He had a great fastball, which was practically unhittable, but you could go up looking for the fastball and have a chance. When he got to where he could get his curveball over the plate, you had practically no chance.

He came up in 1955. He was only twenty-two and he won 16 games and led the league in strikeouts with 245. The next year, he won 20 and led the league again in strikeouts with 263. So here he was just twenty-three and he had already won 36 games and struck out 508 batters. As a comparison, Koufax didn't win more than 11 games or strike out more than 200 batters until his seventh season, when he was twenty-five, and he made the Hall of Fame. I believe Score would have made the Hall of Fame if he hadn't gotten hurt.

It happened in 1957, in May. We were in Cleveland and Score was pitching against us and Gil McDougald hit a wicked line drive back to the box. I don't know if it was simply that the ball was hit so hard, or if Score lost it, or if his follow-through made him take his eye off the ball, but he never picked up the flight of the ball and it hit him right in the face. I was in our dugout when it happened and I remember hearing *pow—pow,* the bat hitting the ball, then the ball hitting Score. Just like that, almost with no time in between.

Score fell to the ground, and players and trainers came rushing out there. Some people thought he was dead. I thought it knocked his eye out. There was blood all over the mound. They rushed Score to the hospital and I remember McDougald was very upset about it. For a long time, it was touch and go about Score's eye, and his future in baseball, and I remember Gil crying and saying that if anything happened to Score, he was going to quit baseball.

Score recovered and he even came back to pitch, but he never was the same again. He lasted five more seasons and this guy who won 36 games in his first two seasons, wound up winning only 17 more for five seasons. It was a tragedy. What a waste of a great talent.

I still see Herb once in a while. He's a broad-caster for Indian games and doing very well. But he could have been a Hall of Famer.

They called us the Bronx Bombers, but against Cleveland's staff I felt lucky if I came out of there with four hits in a four-game series.

After we beat Lemon, Wynn shut us out on a three-hitter, then Lemon came back on one day's rest and beat us, 5–1, on a six-hitter. That's how good they were and how unwilling they were to concede anything even when they were behind by ten games.

In the fourth game of the series, we faced Score and lost again, 4–0. A four-hitter. So we won the first game of the four-game series, then lost the next three, and in those three games, we scored just one run and had only thirteen hits and I had only one hit in ten at bats. Less than two weeks before, we had led the league by eleven games. Now, our lead was down to seven. It was only the first week of August, we still had about fifty games to play and we knew the Indi-ans, with their great pitching, were going to be tough.

· · ·

One of the toughest things in baseball is to pull out of a tailspin. Baseball is a game of streaks. It's also a mental game. Funny thing about streaks: once you go on a winning streak, you think you're never going to lose another game, and once you go on a losing streak, you think you're never going to win again. That's what we were going through. Good thing we had such a big cushion of a lead.

We left Cleveland and went to Detroit and lost our fourth straight. Whitey lost the game, and to make matters worse, he got hurt when he took a comebacker on his left hand and had to leave the game. I was worried about Slick. If we lost him for any period of time, we might be in trouble. Our lead was seven games. Meanwhile, in the National League race, the Dodgers had been on a hot streak. From six games behind Milwaukee in late July, they were now only two games out.

We lost our second straight to the Tigers, and fifth straight overall, 5–4, even though I had three hits, including my thirty-fifth and thirty-sixth home runs. But Al Kaline also hit two homers and drove in all five of the Tigers' runs.

Now it was getting serious. The Tigers swept us in three games. We still had a seven-game lead with less than fifty games to play, but our losing streak was now at six games. I hit my thirty-seventh homer, but Kaline burned us again. He hit his twenty-first home run and knocked in three more runs and was gaining ground on me in the race for the league RBI championship. I always liked Kaline. I thought he had a lot of class and was one of the best players of that era. He's in the Hall of Fame and he deserves it.

We took our six-game losing streak into Boston, where Casey took a bit of a gamble. We brought up a young pitcher from the minor leagues and started him against the Red Sox in Fenway Park. The kid's name was Ralph Terry, another Oklahoman, just like me.

I was familiar with Terry. I remembered seeing him pitch for Chelsea High School in Oklahoma against my twin brothers, Ray and Roy. Terry was a tall, skinny kid who could throw hard. The Yankees signed him right out of high school and he played a couple of years, then moved up to Denver in the AAA American Association. He was 13–4 for Denver, which was managed by Ralph Houk at the time, when the Yankees called him up and put him right to work against the Red Sox.

Terry beat the Red Sox, 4–3, with help from Tommy Byrne, to end our losing streak at six games. Terry would become one of the mainstays on our pitching staff over the next few years. He was also, unfortunately, the guy who threw the pitch that Bill Mazeroski hit for a home run to beat us in the 1960 World Series. That was the worst I ever felt after losing a game.

We lost that World Series to the Pirates even though we were clearly a much better team. The scores of the games point that out, I think. We won three games in that World Series by scores of 16–3, 10–0 and 12–0. The Pirates won four games by scores of 6–4, 3–2, 5–2 and 10–9. So we outscored them for the Series, 55–27, and outhit them, 91–60. But the rules say you have to win four games to be world champions and that's what the Pirates did. I never felt so bad in my life. I cried all the way home on the plane from Pittsburgh to New York.

That was the only time in my professional career that I actually cried after losing. It was also the only time in my career I felt like hitting one of my teammates. I won't tell you who it was because he's a good guy and he's still a friend, but after we had been beaten by the Pirates and we were all feeling lousy, on the flight home this particular player said, "What's the big deal? It's only a game."

Maybe he was just trying to comfort us, I don't know, but it was the wrong thing to say. And I really felt like hitting that player. Only a game? Was he kidding? That's not the way Yankees talked and, as it turned out, he wasn't a Yankee much longer after that.

Mazeroski's home run also was the low point of Ralph Terry's career, but then in 1962 he won 23 games and 2 more in the World Series and he pitched in one of the most exciting games I ever played in.

We were tied with the Giants in the World Series, three games apiece, and Terry pitched the seventh game in Candlestick Park. We scored a run off Jack Sanford in the fifth inning when the Giants' manager, Alvin Dark, played the infield back with none out and the bases loaded. He figured the Giants, with hitters like Willie Mays, Willie McCovey, Orlando Cepeda and Felipe Alou, would score against Terry. So Dark was willing to concede one run to stay out of the big inning.

Moose scored when Tony Kubek hit into a double play to give us a 1–0 lead. And that's how it stayed going into the bottom of the ninth.

Matty Alou led off the ninth and beat out a

bunt for a hit. Terry then struck out Matty's brother, Felipe, and Chuck Hiller and now we were only one out away from winning our second straight world championship. But Mays sliced a drive into the right-field corner that looked like it would score Alou from first with the tying run. Then Roger Maris made one of the greatest plays I've ever seen; one of those plays that never show up in the box score but save a game and are remembered forever by the rest of the team. That's why Roger was so great, because he was a complete player. A great fielder, a great arm and a thinking ballplayer.

Roger got into the corner fast, picked up the ball and in one motion fired it to second baseman Bobby Richardson, the cutoff man. Alou couldn't score. He'd have been out by ten feet.

Now with runners on second and third and Willie McCovey coming up, Ralph Houk went out to the mound to talk to Terry. I thought Houk was either going to tell Terry to walk McCovey, who was a left-handed hitter, and pitch to Orlando Cepeda, a right-handed hitter, or going to bring in a left-hander to face McCovey. Houk didn't do either thing. He left Terry in to pitch to McCovey, going against the percentages. Why? Ralph never said. It might have been just a hunch, but who was I to question Houk? I did hear later that Terry talked Houk into letting him pitch to McCovey.

"I can get this guy," Terry said.

So Houk left Terry in to pitch to McCovey, and Ralph had hardly got back to the bench when McCovey hit this tremendous shot down the right-field line, clear over everything. At first it looked like a three-run homer and we were beat. But the ball sailed foul.

Maybe Houk was having second thoughts about leaving Terry in right then, but he stayed with Terry. Two pitches later, McCovey hit a vicious line drive to the right side. It looked like it would sail over Richardson's head for a single and two runs would score and we'd be beat. But Bobby jumped and caught it and we were world champions.

Terry would win 107 games in the big leagues and his first one would be against the Red Sox when he came up from the minor leagues to break our six-game losing streak. That was typical of the Yankees in those days. They had such depth at every position, they could call a player up from the minor leagues and he would contribute.

· · ·

It was a great relief, a weight off our shoulders, when Terry beat the Red Sox and ended our losing streak at six games. We felt so good that Billy and I decided to go out that night and celebrate. Not that we ever needed an excuse to party.

We went out to eat, then we had a few drinks and the next thing we knew it was 11:50. We had a midnight curfew, so we hustled out of the place and grabbed a cab back to the Kenmore Hotel, which was only a few minutes away. Wouldn't you know it, we got caught in a traffic jam, and when we pulled up in front of the Kenmore, it was 12:05. We were late and that meant a pretty stiff fine if Casey saw us.

We walked up the steps to the front door of the hotel and we could see Casey in the lobby talking to a couple of writers. As long as there was one writer around, Casey would always stand there and talk. Now we were in trouble.

So Billy and I went around to the back door, but it was locked. Down an alley, we spotted an open transom about one story up and that gave Billy an idea.

"I'll get up on your shoulders," he said, "and climb through the window, then I'll come around and open the door for you."

I had on this brand-new sharkskin suit that I

really liked and I wasn't too thrilled about Billy climbing on my shoulders. But I figured I had no other choice, so I grabbed a garbage can in the alley and stood on it and let Billy climb up on my shoulders and let himself in through the transom.

Then I could hear Billy inside, trying to get the door open, and then I didn't hear him anymore. The next thing I knew, I heard a voice coming from the transom. It's Billy.

"Hey, Mick," he said. "That door has a lock and a chain. I can't get it open. I'll see you tomorrow."

He left me there and then I had to stack about three or four of those garbage cans and climb up to try to get through the transom. And I kept falling off the cans onto the ground. I finally made it through the transom, but I had lettuce and tomatoes and all kinds of garbage all over my brand-new suit.

I finally got up to the room and there was Billy, fast asleep.

We split the two-game series in Boston and headed for Washington. We swept two from the Senators and scored twenty-seven runs in the two games and I hit my thirty-eighth and thirty-ninth homers. Then we came home and took two out of three from Baltimore. I was getting hot again. I had three hits in a doubleheader against the Orioles, including my forty-first home run. I was eleven games ahead of Babe Ruth and my batting average was .371. Best of all, we had opened an eight-and-a-half-game lead over Cleveland.

The Red Sox came into Yankee Stadium for a three-game series beginning August 14. The Red Sox in town meant a big crowd, as always. It also meant a chance to see Ted Williams hit again. He was thirty-seven years old and he missed a lot of games because of little injuries, but the guy could still hit. He is still the last man in baseball to hit over .400; he batted .406 in 1941. After a slow start in 1956 Ted got hot and now he was closing in on my lead in the race for the batting championship. I had never won a batting title and I wanted it very badly. But I knew Williams was going to make it tough for me to win it, no matter how old he was. I would rather be chased by any player but him. But then, if I was going to lose the batting championship, I wanted to lose it to the greatest hitter who ever lived.

There were more than fifty-two thousand people in Yankee Stadium for the first game of

the Red Sox series, including President Eisenhower. I didn't know what it was, but it seemed
like every time President Eisenhower came to a
game, I hit a home run. I know I wasn't trying to
hit a home run for him, but maybe just the fact
that he was there got my adrenaline going a little
more and I hit better. He was running for reelec-
tion in October and all the polls predicted he was
going to beat Adlai Stevenson again for another
four-year term. But I wondered, if he lost, would
he consider traveling around with us as my personal good-luck charm?

We bombed the Red Sox, 12–2. Johnny
Kucks won his sixteenth and, with my good-luck
charm in the stands, I went three for three to
raise my average to .376. Williams was one for
three and was batting .354. I also hit my forty-
second home run, putting me thirteen games
ahead of Babe Ruth. With Ike's help, maybe I
could break the Babe's record.

Our winning streak went to four games, our
lead to ten and a half games over the Indians,
which should have been cause for celebration. It
wasn't. In winning our fourth straight, 6–4, over
Boston, Whitey's shoulder stiffened up in the
fourth inning and he had to leave the game, cost-
ing him a chance for a win. It would come back
to haunt him later in the season. But right now

we were mainly concerned about Whitey's shoulder. We might not need him to win the pennant, but we sure were going to need him in the World Series.

Through the latter part of August, our streakiness continued. I went through three consecutive hitless games and my average tumbled from the .370s into the low .360s. What was once a commanding lead in the batting race was now a slim lead, and Ted Williams was always a threat to get hot and overtake me.

Frustrating game, baseball. When you're on a hot streak, hitting seems like the easiest thing in the world. The ball comes up there looking like a great big balloon and you think you're never going to make out. But when you cool off and go into a slump, the ball comes up there looking like a golf ball and you get the feeling you're never going to get another hit. That's the reason hitting a baseball has been said to be the toughest single thing to do in sports. In what other activity can you fail seven out of ten times and still be considered a success?

While I was slumping, we went into another of our frequent slides, our lead cut to seven and a half games as the Indians were hanging tough. We faced Herb Score again and again he showed why he would have been a Hall of Famer, shutting us out, 3–0, striking out eleven and holding us to only two hits. I had one of the hits off Score, a single in the ninth. But we didn't get our first hit until the eighth, when Elston Howard doubled. A double for Elston Howard would be an inside-the-park home run for most other players. That's the one thing Ellie couldn't do on a baseball field—run.

Ellie was quickly becoming one of the best players on the team. He already was one of the best guys.

He was from St. Louis, a quiet, humble man, a good friend and an outstanding ballplayer. I first met Ellie in spring training in 1955, and I immediately took a liking to him. He had a tremendous minor-league record and the Yankees brought him along slowly. You have to remember, that was only eight years after Jackie Robinson broke the color line with the Dodgers and not every team had a black player. The Yankees were one of the last to get a black. I don't know if it was some kind of prejudice in the front office or if they just couldn't find a good black player.

They had Vic Power, who was from Puerto Rico, and was black, and when the Yankees traded him to the Athletics, there was a lot of stuff in the papers about them being prejudiced. I don't think that was it at all. Power was very flashy and outspoken and he just wasn't the type of player the Yankees liked back then, black or white. Besides, Power was a first baseman and the team looked like it would be set at first base for years with Moose Skowron.

So Ellie came up and he was the first black player the Yankees ever had, and that had to be added pressure on him besides just trying to make the team and playing in the major leagues. But he took it in stride, and because he was such a good guy, he was immediately accepted by all the guys.

When he came up, Ellie was an outfielder/first baseman, but the Yankees' plan was to convert him to a catcher and slowly break him in to replace Yogi, who was getting older. In his first season, 1955, Ellie caught only nine games and played the outfield seventy-five games. He batted .290, had 10 homers and 43 RBIs and really helped us win the pennant. In 1956, he played the outfield in sixty-five games and caught twenty-six. He kept catching more and more, until he became our regular catcher in 1961 and one of the best in the game.

Ellie was an excellent defensive catcher with

a great throwing arm and he became Whitey's accomplice when Whitey began to bend the rules a little late in his career. Whitey liked to get a baseball with a nick in it that would make the ball move a lot. But he knew he couldn't stand on the mound and slash a baseball because the other manager and coaches and players and the umpires were watching him like hawks.

That's when Ellie decided to help Whitey out. He had one of the clasps on his shin guards sharpened so that it could cut a nick in the baseball. He would "accidentally" drop a ball, and as he picked it up, he would rub it across the clasp and there would be a nice little nick in the ball for Whitey. Nobody ever figured out what was going on.

There were no black people in the part of Oklahoma where I grew up. No blacks working in the zinc mines. So I never knew any until I started playing ball and I think I had no feeling about them one way or another. I really don't remember having any prejudices against blacks then, or now. The fact that the first black teammate I had was Elston Howard, and he was such a terrific guy, had something to do with my later attitude toward blacks.

When Ellie first joined the team, I didn't

think anything about it. I figured if he could play, I was glad he was going to be there.

We got to be very close, me and Ellie. In the early years, when we would play exhibition games in Florida, or were heading north through the South, we would stop to eat and Ellie wouldn't be allowed to go in with the rest of the team because he was black. He'd have to sit in the bus and wait for the other guys, and I used to stay on the bus with him. Not because I was such a champion for civil rights, but because Ellie always had better food. These black families would pack him some food for the trip, knowing he couldn't go in restaurants, and we'd be on the bus eating barbecued chicken and ribs and the other guys were in there eating hamburgers.

After he quit playing, Ellie became a coach for the Yankees. And he was so loyal to the organization and the manager that he coached for a long time, under a lot of different managers. We remained friends through the years. Billy was close to him too. Billy had Ellie as a coach when he was manager of the Yankees and he trusted Ellie and considered him a loyal assistant.

Billy and I used to tease Ellie a lot. When we got into a hotel on the road, we'd tell Ellie to deliver our bags to our room. People who didn't know us might think that was cruel of Billy and me, or that this was racial. But we were just having fun and Ellie understood. You don't tease a guy unless you like him and both Billy and I were very fond of Ellie.

When Ellie got sick and was in the hospital, Billy and I used to go and visit him as often as we could. We liked to joke with him to try to keep his spirits up. Next to his family, Billy and I may have been the last ones to see Ellie alive. We went to the hospital to see him and I put a sign on his door that said BRING ME SOME WATERMELON. Ellie laughed harder than anybody else.

Ellie died in 1980, just before Christmas. He was only fifty-one. It was one of the saddest days of my life.

So anyway, we continued on a win-one, lose-one course through the second half of August, but our big lead stayed pretty much intact. Meanwhile, I was in a horrendous slump, only three hits for thirty-one at bats. My batting average slipped to .358, and although I was still five games ahead of Babe Ruth, I had gone eight days without a homer.

I finally broke out of my slump with three hits in the second game of a doubleheader against the White Sox on August 23, including my forty-third homer. On that day, I witnessed one of the greatest exhibitions of hitting I have

ever seen. Nellie Fox, the Chicago second baseman, that little man with the big chew, rapped
out seven straight hits, line drives all over the
place.

The Yankees held their annual Old-Timers'
Day on August 25, something I always looked
forward to. It meant Joe DiMaggio would come
back and a lot of the guys I played with when I
broke in. Also some great Yankees who were before my time, like Bill Dickey, Red Ruffing and
Charlie Keller. I even got to see some real old-
timers from other teams, like Ty Cobb and Charlie Gehringer and Mickey Cochrane, my dad's
favorite player. That's why he named me
Mickey, because he admired Mickey Cochrane
so much. Before I was born, my dad decided I
was going to be a boy, I was going to be named
Mickey and I was going to be a ballplayer. He
even put a little baseball mitt in my crib, which
has now become a famous story.

I never got to see Cochrane play, but I had
heard his name and the names of Gehringer and
a lot of guys from my dad for as long as I could
remember.

Old-Timers' Day is always a happy occasion,

but this one wasn't. Before the game, George Weiss, our general manager, called Phil Rizzuto into his office and told him the club was going to make a move. They had a chance to get Enos Slaughter back from Kansas City and they wanted him for the stretch run and the World Series. Weiss asked Rizzuto who he would get rid of from our roster to make room for Slaughter.

Phil figured because he was a veteran and such a good judge of talent, Weiss wanted his opinion. So he said, "Well, I think we could get rid of a pitcher."

And Weiss just shook his head no.

"We could send Billy Hunter down," Rizzuto said.

"No," Weiss said. "I don't think so."

"How about Jerry Lumpe?"

Again Weiss shook his head. By this time, Rizzuto was getting the message. Weiss knew the move he wanted to make and that's why he had called Phil into his office. Finally, Weiss dropped the bomb.

"We have no choice, Phil," he said. "We've got to release you to make room on our roster for Slaughter."

Rizzuto was crushed. He never expected it. There was such confusion because of the old-timers, I never did get to see Phil, but I was told

later that he was in tears. He was insulted because he felt the Yankees didn't treat him right
after all those years, and he was humiliated that
he got the word on Old-Timers' Day, in front of
DiMaggio and all his old teammates.

He packed his stuff quickly and got out of
there in a hurry before he had to face any of his
teammates. He later told me that if it hadn't been
for his old second-base partner, George
Stirnweiss, who happened to be there for Old-
Timers' Day, he didn't know how he would have
gotten home; that's how upset he was.

For a long time, Scooter was very bitter toward the Yankees, especially Weiss. He even
took a job broadcasting New York Giant games
for the rest of the season. But getting released
turned out to be a blessing in disguise for him.
After the season, the Yankees brought him back
to join their broadcast team, working with Mel
Allen and Red Barber. Phil started broadcasting
in the 1957 season, and he's been there ever
since, almost thirty-five years as a Yankee broad-
caster. So he traveled with us through my last
twelve years with the team and we remained
good friends.

After I retired, I got to do some radio and TV
work for the Yankees and I worked alongside
Scooter. He was very helpful to me and he re-

mains one of my favorite all-time characters. He has these fears of so many things. He's afraid of flying, he's afraid of lightning and he's afraid of any kind of crawly bugs or insects. Naturally, the more he showed his fear, the more we played jokes on him, like putting bugs and insects in the broadcast booth just to see his reaction.

Another thing about Phil is his reputation for leaving the ballpark early. He always finds an excuse to get out of there in the seventh or eighth inning and often boasts he's across the George Washington Bridge and home before the game ends.

Above all, my memory of Phil Rizzuto is that he was one of the best shortstops I ever saw. A strong little guy and a great competitor. It's a shame he's not in the Hall of Fame. He certainly belongs there. Let me put it this way: if Pee Wee Reese is in, then Phil should be. I always admired and respected Pee Wee and thought he was a good guy and a terrific shortstop. But I think Phil was just as good. Believe me, I saw them both and there is no way Reese was better. I wish they could have gone into the Hall of Fame together.

Ted Williams used to say that if the Red Sox had Rizzuto in the forties and fifties, Boston would have won all those pennants in those years and not the Yankees. And I agree with him.

· · ·

I got hot toward the end of August and continued to hang in there against Ruth. I hit my forty-fifth and forty-sixth home runs against Kansas City and raised my average back to .367 and we kept our lead at eight games.

On the last day of August, we were in Washington to play the Senators and President Eisenhower attended the game. My favorite ballpark to hit in and my good-luck charm. How could I miss?

Before the game, I met the President and he told me, "I hope you hit a home run, but I hope the Senators win."

I hit a home run, my forty-seventh, and we won, 6–4. Jim Lemon, the Senators' tall, right-handed slugger, hit three homers off Whitey to account for all four of Washington's runs. We were leading by two going into the bottom of the ninth when the Senators put two runners on base and Casey came to the mound. From center field, I could see Whitey and Casey having this long discussion. Not an argument, but a lot of talk for what seemed to me to be an obvious situation.

Later, Whitey told me what was said.

"Casey came out," Whitey said, "and I told

him, 'I can get this guy, Case. Let me pitch to him.'

"And Casey just looked at me and said, 'Are you friggin crazy? The guy already hit three homers off you.' "

So Casey called in Tom Morgan and he got Lemon out to win the game.

I had finished the month of August with 47 homers. I needed only 13 more in twenty-five games to tie Babe Ruth, 14 to beat him. I had a chance. But I wasn't kidding myself. A lot of guys had come into September with a chance to break the Babe's record and couldn't do it. Guys like Hank Greenberg, Jimmie Foxx and Johnny Mize all were far ahead of Ruth's pace going into September. But September always beat them. The year he hit 60, the Babe hit 17 in the month of September and that's what killed off all the challengers—17 homers in a month, plus all the pressure. That stopped everybody. Until Roger Maris.

8

The
Triple
Crown

$\mathcal{I}$ must have talked myself into a September jinx, because I started out the month in another of those awful slumps. Couldn't get a home run if the pitcher told me what was coming. Which reminds me of the times that actually happened. Only twice in my career.

The first time was when I was just a young player. It was 1952 and I had already hit some long home runs. We were playing the Philadelphia Athletics and they had this catcher from Georgia named Joe Tipton who used to love to see me hit long home runs. One day, I came to bat right-handed and Tipton looks at me and says, in a low voice, so the umpire couldn't hear him, "Hi, big guy, what would you like to have?"

"How about a change-up?" I said.

"You got it," Tipton said.

Sure enough, the first pitch is a change-up and I hit it deep into the stands for a home run. I round the bases and as I get to home plate, Tipton takes his mask off, looks at me and winks.

The only other time something like that happened to me was late in the 1968 season, my final year. We were in Detroit. I had 534 home runs, which tied me with Jimmie Foxx for third on the all-time list at the time. Denny McLain was pitching for the Tigers and he always was kind of a flaky guy. We also had a pretty good relationship.

I always liked Denny. Not only was he a great pitcher for a few years, he seemed like such a fun guy, although I didn't hang out with him and never spent a lot of time with him. I'd see him when we played the Tigers and he would come over and talk, or in an All-Star Game. But that's about it.

I really felt bad when he got in that trouble, associating with gamblers, and went to jail. I know that had to kill him because he was always such a free spirit. I know being in jail must have been tough on him and his family. But he served his sentence and he's out now and I really hope he's put all that trouble behind him and can live a normal and useful life. He deserves that for all he went through.

Denny was having a spectacular season. He would wind up winning 31 games. Baseball hadn't had a 30-game winner since Dizzy Dean in 1934 and they haven't had one since McLain.

On this particular day, McLain had us beat by about six runs when I came to bat for the last time. And Denny calls his catcher, Bill Freehan, out from behind the plate. They're standing about five or six feet away from me and I think I hear Denny tell Freehan, "This is probably his last time at bat in Detroit. Let's let him hit one."

I couldn't believe my ears. I wasn't sure I heard right, so when Freehan settled behind the plate, I asked him.

"Hey, Bill, did I hear what I think I heard? He wants me to hit one?"

"Yeah," Freehan said. "He's not going to work on you. He's just going to throw you fastballs."

I still wasn't sure he wasn't setting me up, because, as I said, Denny always was kind of flaky and I didn't know if I could trust him. Besides, even if I was convinced he was telling the truth, that he really wanted me to hit one, there was no guarantee I was going to do it. There never is. You could put a ball on a tee, it's no cinch you're going to hit it out of the park. A lot of times, in batting practice, you're trying to hit the ball out of the ballpark and you can't do it.

I know you've seen those home-run-hitting contests. A guy gets to take his own batting practice pitcher, gets to ask for the ball wherever he wants it, and still most of the time they don't hit the ball out. So it's not that easy to hit one out, even if you know what's coming.

Anyway, the first pitch came in, a batting practice fastball, right over the heart of the plate, and I just took it. And Denny looks at me and shrugs as if to say, "Hey, man, what are you looking at it for?"

Now I know he's going to let me hit one. The next pitch comes in, another fastball down the middle, but I swung too hard trying to hit it out and I popped it foul, out of the stands behind the plate. The next pitch is another fastball down the middle and this one I really got into and hit it into the upper deck for my 535th home run to pass Foxx.

As I'm going around the bases, I can see out

of the corner of my eye that Denny is sort of smiling. When I pass third, I look right at him and he gives me a big wink.

Our next batter is Joe Pepitone, talk about flaky guys, and he sees what's going on, so he must have figured McLain was in a generous mood. He steps up to the plate and he puts his hand right over the middle of the plate as if to say, "I'll take one right here." With his first pitch, McLain knocked Pepi down.

Now in September, with a chance to catch Babe Ruth, what I needed was a Denny McLain to give me a pitch I could hit out of the park. Instead, I was struggling, hit by the September jinx and the pressure of Ruth's record.

We played the first two games of the month in Griffith Stadium, against the Washington Senators, the team I had killed all season. But I failed to hit a home run. When I don't get a home run against the Senators in two games in Griffith Stadium, you know that's a bad sign. Where was President Eisenhower when I really needed him? I'm sure he had nothing more important to do than come to the ball game so I could hit a home run.

Not only didn't I get a homer, I didn't get a hit in the two games and we lost both of them to the Senators.

A week later, Washington came into Yankee Stadium for a three-game weekend series and my slump continued. I was one for 11 in the three games, a single in the middle game of the three, which we won, 16–2, with twenty hits. Now I had gone eight games in September without a home run. I had fallen behind Ruth's pace, and my chances of breaking his record were fading fast.

When you get into any kind of a slump, you start to press, and the more you press, the worse you hit, so it becomes a catch-22. You slump, so you press, and when you press, you slump some more. The only way to get out of a slump is to relax and do things naturally. But that's easier said than done.

We beat the Senators, 2–1, on Sunday, September 9, with Whitey winning it to raise his record to 17–5. Like I said, he'd never won 20 in his career and he wanted it very badly. With seventeen games left, we figured he'd get four more starts, so he still had a chance for 20. But my chances of catching Babe Ruth were now remote. That was O.K. We opened an eleven-game lead and we were on the verge of clinching the American League pennant.

Whitey went home to his wife, Joan, after the game, and I don't remember where Billy was, so I decided to stay in and get room service and watch some television. I turned on *The Ed Sullivan Show* and saw a twenty-one-year-old guitar player and singer who had been a truck driver before he turned to music. His name was Elvis Presley and he was making his first appearance on *The Ed Sullivan Show*. I had heard of Elvis, but I had never seen him.

He had been making quite a name for himself. I always loved country music. Still do. People like Merle Haggard, Hank Williams and Willie Nelson. They were some of my favorites. Also Conway Twitty, Charlie Daniels, Hank Williams, Jr., and a lot of the new ones like Randy Travis and Clint Black and too many others to mention.

I always liked Elvis' music, and I still like to listen to it. I wish I'd met him. I think maybe we would have had some things in common, both country boys. But I never did get the opportunity to meet him.

· · ·

Not only wasn't I hitting home runs, I wasn't hitting anything. I was in danger of losing my lead in the race for the batting championship. Another hitless game extended my slump to twelve at bats without a hit and my average had fallen to .352, the lowest it was all season. I could almost feel the hot breath of Ted Williams on the back of my neck and Al Kaline was closing in on my RBI lead. I was being chased by a couple of all-time greats. Williams was just three points behind me at .349. And my RBI lead over Kaline had shrunk to 118 to 116.

On September 13, I broke out of my slump with two hits, including my forty-eighth homer. But I was four games behind Ruth and only a miracle would help me catch him. But Whitey won his eighteenth and his chances of winning 20 were looking very good.

Three days later, we played a doubleheader in Cleveland, and when we won the first game, we eliminated the Indians. The White Sox were still alive, but just barely. I hit my forty-ninth homer, leaving me 11 away from Ruth with ten games to play. Do you believe in miracles?

The next day was a travel day, another train trip to Chicago, where we would have a shot at clinching the pennant. To help pass the time, I grabbed a newspaper and read the sports pages. I noticed that the Dodgers had moved into first place by half a game over the Braves. That race was going to go right down to the end.

We clinched the pennant in Chicago on September 18, our fifth American League pennant in my six years with the Yankees; their seventh pennant in eight seasons with Casey Stengel as manager.

Whatever you do, don't get the idea that Casey was a push-button manager. True, he had good players, but he also worked hard to get the most out of them. One year, we had so many injuries he had to keep patching here and patching there. He won with hitting and he won with pitching. He lost players and he still won. Casey deserves as much credit for those championships as anyone wants to give him.

Even though we were way in front and had known for about three weeks that we couldn't be caught, clinching day is always a thrill. It was a great game, Whitey Ford for us against Billy Pierce, already a 20-game winner, for the White Sox. Both pitched great and we went into the eleventh inning tied, 2–2. I homered off Pierce to give us a 3–2 lead, the ball going over the roof in left center. It was the longest ball ever hit in Comiskey Park. They measured it at 550 feet, and now that the Sox have played the last game there, that's one record I can be sure will never be surpassed.

After my home run put us ahead, Whitey got them out in the bottom of the eleventh and we won, 3–2. It was Whitey's nineteenth victory. We had nine games left, so he could possibly get two starts, and he needed to win one of them to finally win 20 in a season.

My home run off Pierce was number 50. That had been done only twelve times in the history of baseball and by only eight different players (Babe Ruth did it four times, Jimmie Foxx and Ralph Kiner twice each, and the others were Hack Wilson, Hank Greenberg, Johnny Mize and Willie Mays). It also meant I was the only Yankee other than Babe Ruth to hit 50 home runs in a season. It was a proud moment for me.

There was champagne in the clubhouse to celebrate winning the pennant, most of it spilled and squirted around the room instead of being drunk. I never was much for clubhouse celebrations. I just didn't get into that kind of stuff. I just got me a beer, found a quiet place, maybe in the trainer's room, and just relaxed and thought about what we had just done. We did our partying that night when Whitey, Billy and I went on the town. We had two days off before going into Boston for a three-game weekend series with the Red Sox, so we could really live it up.

With the pennant already wrapped up and my chances of catching Babe Ruth just about gone, the thing the fans were most involved in during our three games in Boston was the batting race. Ted Williams was on a hot streak, and when we went into Boston, he had taken over the league lead in hitting. He was at .355 and I was at .350. But I had a tremendous advantage.

In order to qualify for the batting title, a player had to have 400 at bats. Williams had only 372 at bats, meaning he needed 28 at bats in eight games to qualify. It was possible, but just barely.

There was a technicality that still gave him a chance even if he failed to get the necessary at bats. Let's say he finished with 395 at bats. They would arbitrarily add those five at bats, without hits, and if his average was still the highest, he would be awarded the batting crown. So all I had to do was stay within a point or two and I would win the title, because it didn't look like

Williams was going to get his 400 at bats. But I didn't want to win it that way. I wanted to finish with a higher batting average than he had, regardless of the number of at bats.

The Red Sox beat us, 13–7, in the first game of the series, which meant they all came to bat a lot. But Williams was always too proud to swing at bad pitches, even if it meant helping his chances of winning the batting title, so he got a walk and had only four official at bats. He got two hits and his average went from .355 to .356. I had three for five and raised my average from .350 to .353. I also hit my fifty-first home run and it was the number 183 for the team, setting an American League record.

I regained the batting lead in the second game of the series. We beat the Red Sox, 2–1, and I had two hits in three at bats to raise my average to .3542. Williams batted four times and was hitless. His average was .3526.

That was the good news. The bad news was that I pulled a muscle in my right thigh and was probably going to have to sit out a few games. I didn't want to sit by and watch Williams take the batting title from me and not be able to do anything about it. I wanted to be out there winning it or losing it myself. But Casey argued that the World Series was more important than any batting title and he didn't want me to aggravate my thigh and have to miss the Series. I couldn't argue with him.

The Series was going to start in less than two weeks, and it *was* more important than any batting title, although we still didn't know who we were going to play. The Dodgers and Braves were in an exact tie for first place in the National League race.

I sat out the third game of the series in Boston, but Casey used me as a pinch hitter for Hank Bauer in the ninth inning and I singled to raise my average to .356. Williams was hitless in three at bats. His average dropped to .350. There was still a week left in the season. I was nursing a pulled thigh muscle and the Red Sox were scheduled to come to Yankee Stadium for the final three games of the season. I began to get the feeling that the batting race was going to go down to the last day. Maybe the last at bat.

We went to Baltimore, our last stop before the Red Sox series at home. I still wasn't able to start, but I got to pinch-hit. In the first game against the Orioles, I walked. Williams had an off day. So it was status quo.

In the second game, I pinch-hit in the fifth inning and fouled out. I lost a point and my average was .355. Williams was one for four and he dropped a point, to .349. But now I had a new problem. Al Kaline knocked in a run to give him 124. I had 127. Kaline was healthy and I wasn't. He could have a big day or two and pass me in RBIs. Williams could get hot and pass me in batting. My home-run lead was safe, but I was in danger of not getting the Triple Crown I wanted so badly.

It's funny, but just recently I was looking at some old films and there was this interview that I did in the spring of 1956. I'm in a dugout, possibly in Florida, and I'm saying that my goal for the season was to lead the league in home runs, RBIs and batting average, and for the Yankees to win another world championship.

That was pretty bold of me to predict a Triple Crown, now that I think of it. It had been years since it was done and I must have seemed a little boastful to say I wanted to do it. But since I had put myself out on the limb, I figured I might as well shoot for it. Nobody would remember that interview if I failed. At least I hoped they wouldn't.

When I hit all those home runs early, I knew nobody would catch me for the home-run title, if

I stayed healthy. I didn't even give much of a thought about winning the RBI title because I got off to such a big lead. It wasn't until late in the season that I became aware of Al Kaline gaining on me.

The category that I worried about was the batting title, and that was only because Ted Williams was around. Anytime Ted was playing, he had to be the favorite to win the batting championship, and 1956 was no exception.

The third game of the series was a heartbreaker. Whitey was going for his twentieth win and he wanted it badly. Pitching against him was a twenty-one-year-old named Charlie Beamon, making his first major-league start. I wanted to play to help Whitey win his twentieth, but Stengel wouldn't let me.

The Orioles scored a run early, but we figured one run wouldn't stand up. No way a kid making his first major-league start was going to shut us out. We were wrong.

We got only four hits in the game and Whitey got two of them. I got my chance to hit in the seventh. Whitey was on third with one out and Casey sent me up to bat for Joe Collins. I never wanted to get hold of one so much. Maybe I tried too hard, because I popped one up just behind second base. Later, I kidded Whitey. I told him he should have tagged up and scored.

- We lost the game, 1–0. It meant that we couldn't win 100 games for the season. Worse than that, it meant that Whitey wouldn't win 20 unless he came back four days later to pitch the final game of the season against the Red Sox. Casey gave him his choice. He could have tried for his twentieth. But Whitey said no, the World Series was more important than winning 20 games, which is what I would have expected him to say. Whitey always was a team player, more interested in winning championships than any personal glory.

Beamon didn't stay around the major leagues long. I don't know if he had arm trouble or what, but he was gone a year later. He won only three games in his career, but one of them cost Whitey a chance to win 20. He would do it later. Like I said earlier, in 1961 he had one of the greatest seasons any pitcher ever had. Ralph Houk put him on a four-day rotation and Whitey was 25–4. But he really wanted to win 20 in 1956.

My pop-up dropped my average another point, down to .354. Williams was two for four that day and he was batting .350 as we prepared for the showdown three-game series in New York.

I was back in the starting lineup for the first game against the Red Sox, which is how I wanted it. I didn't want to be sitting on the bench with the batting title at stake. I had one hit in four at bats, my fifty-second home run. It was a solo shot, giving me 128 RBIs. Kaline had none that day and he remained at 124.

Williams needed nine official at bats to qualify for the batting title. He had three. And all three times, he hit ground balls to Billy at second base. With two of them, Billy started double plays. In his fourth at bat, Williams walked. He was batting .348. I was batting .353.

Casey sat me down in the second game of the series against the Red Sox, a Saturday. I batted in the eighth inning with the bases loaded and walked, so my average stayed at .353 and my RBI total was 129. In Detroit, Kaline had two RBIs, giving him 126.

Our game went thirteen innings. Williams batted six times, which meant he officially qualified for the batting title. But he had only one hit and his average dropped to .345.

That meant that going into the final day of the season, my lead over Williams was eight points, which looked like it was safe, barring miracles. But my lead in RBIs over Kaline was only three, which wasn't safe.

In the National League, the Dodgers went into the next-to-last day of the season trailing Milwaukee by half a game. But the Dodgers swept a doubleheader from Pittsburgh and Milwaukee lost, so the Dodgers took a one-game lead into the final day of the season.

Williams conceded the batting title. He didn't play the final game, finishing with a batting average of .345 at the age of thirty-eight, which is truly amazing. I didn't start either, but I pinch-hit for Jim Coates in the ninth inning and knocked in a run with a ground ball. I finished with a .353 average and the batting title.

Somebody asked Ted after the game how it felt to lose the batting title to me.

"If I could run like that son of a bitch, I'd hit .400 every year," Ted said.

I believe he would have too. I don't know

how many bunt hits and leg hits I got that season, but it must have been at least twenty. I know it was enough to give me my eight-point margin over Williams.

Another thing to consider is that when we played the Red Sox, Williams had to hit against better pitchers than I did.

So I had my batting title. I had clinched the home-run title long ago with my 52, which was twenty more than the runner-up, Vic Wertz of the Indians, and nine more than the National League champion, Duke Snider, of the Dodgers. Billy liked to boast that between us, we hit 61 home runs that year. He hit 9 of them.

Now I had to sweat out word from Detroit to find out if I had won the Triple Crown. Kaline gave it his best shot. He knocked in two runs in the last game to finish with 128, two behind me. I had won the Triple Crown.

I was only the twelfth Triple Crown winner in baseball history. I also led the major leagues in home runs, RBIs and batting average, only the fourth player to do that, and I was in pretty good company. Rogers Hornsby had done it for the St. Louis Cardinals in 1925. Lou Gehrig had done it for the Yankees in 1934. And my idol, Ted Williams, had done it for the Red Sox in 1942.

I was proud of these accomplishments; proud

that I had finally done the things Casey had predicted for me. It was my greatest season in the major leagues, but I wasn't thinking about that at the time. The Dodgers had clinched the National League pennant by beating the Pirates. My Triple Crown season would have meant nothing, it would have been a waste, unless we got the world championship back.

9

The
Rematch

*A*s usual, all of New York was excited about the start of the 1956 World Series, the Yankees and Dodgers meeting for the fourth time in the last five years. The newspapers were calling it "The Rematch," and a lot was made in the press about the Yankees wanting to save face and get their revenge for losing to the Dodgers in the 1955 Series. To be honest, the newspapers made more of that than the players did.

New York City had eight daily newspapers in those days, including one in Brooklyn, and all eight had writers that traveled with each of the three New York teams. In addition, there were a few papers on Long Island and a couple in New Jersey that also sent writers on the road with us, plus several small papers that covered only our home games. So on any road trip we would have anywhere from ten to fifteen writers traveling with us and for home games that number could be as high as twenty or twenty-five. And that didn't include the radio and television reporters.

As you might imagine, the papers were filled with World Series coverage as they competed against one another for stories. And every one of them hit the revenge angle hard.

As for the players, we wanted to win, naturally. It's the World Series. But it wouldn't have mattered if we were playing the Dodgers or Giants or the Milwaukee Braves or the Bad News Bears. We just wanted to be world champions.

Not all of us had such neutral feelings about the Dodgers. Billy hated them. He got caught up in the rivalry between the two teams and he despised the Dodgers. And he hated them even more because they beat us in the 1955 World Series.

Another thing that made Billy so intense was that every year before the Series, when newspapers did a position-by-position comparison of the two teams, the papers would always give the Dodgers a big edge at second base because they had Jackie Robinson and we had Billy Martin. That drove Billy to play harder and to want to win even more.

When the photographers would come around to take pictures of us, they would all flock to Jackie Robinson, Hodges, Snider and Campanella and Whitey, Yogi and me, and they would ignore Billy. That made Billy even madder.

"You better take my picture now," he would tell them, "because I'm going to be the star of this World Series and then I might not be available when you want me."

And damn if he wasn't right. Many players when they try too hard will not play up to their ability. Not Billy. He was just the opposite. When he was motivated by hatred, or revenge, or a personal challenge, he played beyond his ability. As a result, he was an outstanding player in big games and World Series, outplaying Robinson almost every time we met, even though Jackie had much better statistics during the regular season and was a true star who ended up in the Hall of Fame.

In the 1952 Series against the Dodgers, Billy saved it for us with his dramatic catch in the bottom of the seventh inning of the seventh game. We were leading, 4–2, and the Dodgers had the bases loaded with two outs and Jackie Robinson hitting. Jackie hit a high pop to the infield that the wind caught and started blowing back toward home plate. Everybody froze—Joe Collins, the first baseman, Bob Kuzava, the pitcher—and it looked like the ball would fall. All three runners were off with the crack of the bat, and if the ball dropped, at least two runs would have scored and the game would be tied.

All of a sudden Billy realized nobody was going after the ball, so he made a mad dash and he caught it just before it fell. You've probably seen the pictures. Billy's hat has flown off and his arms are outstretched and he's catching the ball at his knees between the pitcher's mound and the third-base foul line.

In the 1953 World Series, Billy set a record for a six-game series with twelve hits. He batted .500, had a double, two triples, two home runs and eight RBIs and he knocked in the winning run in the ninth inning of the sixth game.

In the 1955 World Series, Billy again outplayed Robinson. Billy batted .320; Robinson, .182.

Regardless of Billy's rivalry, I always got along well with Jackie. I admired him because he played hard, but he was a good sport. Casey kept reminding us that our scouts said Jackie liked to take a big turn around the bases and dare you to throw behind him, then he liked to take off for the next base. If he'd hit a single, he'd take a wide turn around first, daring you to throw behind him. The moment you did, he was off for second in a shot.

So Billy and I got together and made it up between us. If Jackie rounded first, I would fake as if I was throwing the ball behind him, then fire the ball to Billy at second. We did it one time. Jackie lined a single to center and I came in and grabbed the ball. I looked up and there he was, taking that wide turn at first. So I wound up like I was going to throw the ball to first, but I held on to the ball. As soon as I bluffed to first, Jackie took off for second. I threw the ball to Billy at second and Robinson was out by twenty feet. Billy slapped the tag on him, real hard. But Jackie never complained.

When we beat them in the 1952 World Series, Robinson came into our clubhouse to congratulate us, which I thought showed a lot of class. He even came over to me and shook my hand and said, "You're going to be a hell of a player." I thought that was real nice of him.

You wouldn't think Robinson would do

something like that, because he had the reputation of being such a fierce competitor who hated to lose. He was, but when he lost, he had enough class to give the other team credit.

The first two games of the 1956 World Series were going to be played in Brooklyn. The middle three games in Yankee Stadium, then the last two, if necessary, back in Brooklyn.

The first game of the Series was on Wednesday afternoon, October 3. The team went over to Brooklyn by bus, leaving from Yankee Stadium. Since the bus had to come through Manhattan on the way to Brooklyn, there was no reason for Billy and me to go all the way up to Yankee Stadium to catch it.

Merlyn had come in for the Series, so Billy took another room in the St. Moritz and we would meet in the coffee shop in the morning, have a quick cup of coffee, then walk over from the hotel to the Yankees' offices in the Squibb Building on Fifth Avenue and the bus would stop and pick us up. Then the bus would head for the FDR Drive, go down to the Brooklyn Bridge, over the bridge into Brooklyn, then through local streets to Ebbets Field.

As we got close to the ballpark, there were crowds of people lined up along the sidewalk. Dodger fans. I don't know how they knew our route or what time we'd be passing, but they were there yelling at us, cursing at us and throwing things at our bus. They were fanatical about their Dodgers and pretty cocky that their team could beat us again.

There never was anything quite like a Brooklyn Dodger fan. They used to have a postgame television show in which a man named Happy Felton, a big, fat guy with glasses who was once a vaudeville comedian, would interview the star of the game. That meant it could be a Dodger or a member of the visiting team.

There was no television studio in those days, so they used to do the show from the back room of a bar across the street from Ebbets Field. It was a typical neighborhood bar and it was always filled with Dodger fans, and if you were chosen as the star of the game and you had to be on the show, you would have to walk through the bar, past all those Dodger fans, to the back.

In 1953, when I hit a grand slam home run in Game 5 of the World Series, I was asked to go on the Happy Felton show. It meant I had to walk through that bar, dressed in my Yankee uniform, right through all those Dodger fans who were angry because I had beaten their team with a grand slam. Let me tell you, I was never so scared in my life.

Ebbets Field was an old ballpark right in the middle of a residential neighborhood. It was quite an interesting place. Very small and cozy. It reminded me a lot of Fenway Park because of its size. It held only about thirty-five thousand people and the fans were right on top of the field, close enough so that you could hear the people razzing you. It was a lot like Fenway Park in its dimensions too, except in reverse.

In Fenway, there's the wall and the big screen in left field. In Ebbets Field, there was a screen on top of the right-field wall, 40 feet high. The wall had a lot of signs, including one advertising a clothing store that offered a free suit to any player who could hit the sign on the fly. The sign was only about five feet high and the right fielder could easily get in front of the sign and catch a line drive hit there, so the clothier gave away very few suits, but he got a great deal of cheap advertising.

In Fenway Park, right field has no screen or wall, just stands. It's only about 300 feet down the right-field line, but it pulls away in right center to about 380. In Ebbets Field, left field had double-decker stands. It was about 350 feet down the line in left, but it didn't pull away toward center field. It was kind of straight across, only about 360 feet to left center and about 390 feet to straightaway center. So it was a very easy park to hit home runs, especially for a right-handed hitter.

When I hit that grand slam against Russ Meyer in Game 5 of the 1953 World Series, it went into the upper deck, but it was just a pop-up that would have been caught in Yankee Stadium. That was the difference between our two parks. A lot of balls that went into the stands in Ebbets Field would have been easy outs in Yankee Stadium. I saw Joe DiMaggio hit about twenty balls in his last year that were caught in Yankee Stadium that would have been home runs in Brooklyn.

That's the reason the Dodgers always loaded their team with right-handed hitters, like Roy Campanella, Gil Hodges, Jackie Robinson, Pee Wee Reese, Andy Pafko and Carl Furillo. Any right-handed hitter was a home-run threat in their ballpark. The only left-handed hitters they had were Duke Snider and Sandy Amoros, and Junior Gilliam, who was a switch hitter. That's also one reason we always had such success against them. Those right-handed hitters would come into Yankee Stadium and hit their best shots that would have been home runs in their ballpark, and we would catch them on the warning track in left field and left center. They got very frustrated hitting in Yankee Stadium. On the other hand, our right-handed hitters would feast in Ebbets Field. After hitting in Yankee Stadium, hitting in Brooklyn was like hitting in a cigar box.

I remember the first time I ever saw Ebbets Field. It was my rookie year, 1951, and we played an exhibition game against the Dodgers in Brooklyn just before the opening of the regular season. I was playing right field at the time because Joe DiMaggio was still around and, naturally, he was the center fielder. Before the game, Casey Stengel took me out to right field and was instructing me on how to play the wall, because it kind of jutted out, slanting down toward home plate, and the ball came off the wall at tricky angles. Also, if the ball hit the screen, it would just die and drop straight down.

So Casey was telling me about the nooks and crannies of the right-field wall at Ebbets Field and I looked at this little old guy, who was in his sixties and walked funny because of a broken leg he had suffered some years before that never healed properly.

"You mean, you played here?" I asked, and from the tone of my voice and the look on my face, I guess it sounded like I couldn't believe it.

"Yeah," Casey said. "Whaddya think, I was born sixty years old?"

Years later, I had the opportunity to look up Casey's playing record and I discovered he was a pretty good player. He played fourteen seasons with the Dodgers, Pirates, Phillies, Giants and Braves and had a lifetime batting average of .284. And I understand he was very fast and an excellent outfielder.

Even as a player, Casey had the reputation of being a clown. The most famous story about him was that he came to bat one day, took off his cap, and a sparrow flew out from under it.

Casey started managing with the Brooklyn Dodgers in 1934. He managed them for three seasons, finishing sixth, fifth and seventh in an eight-team league, and was fired. In 1938, he managed the Boston Braves. He managed there for six seasons, never finishing higher than fifth. In fact, one year a Boston sportswriter wrote that the man who did the most for Boston sports that year was the cabdriver who hit Stengel and broke his leg.

There was nothing in his early managing career that would have led anyone to believe Casey would be so successful with the Yankees. But after he was fired by the Braves, he returned to the minor leagues to manage. He managed Oakland in the Pacific Coast League and was very successful. When Bucky Harris left the Yankees after the 1948 season, the Yankees shocked everybody in baseball by naming Stengel as their manager.

It was Del Webb, team co-owner with Dan Topping, who suggested Stengel as Harris' successor. Webb lived in California, so he followed the Pacific Coast League, and he had great respect for the job Casey did there.

Stengel was fifty-nine at the time. The press ripped the Yankees for their choice. They said Casey was too old, that he was nothing more than a clown and that he was a proven failure in his two previous shots at managing.

That was true, but a manager is only as good as his players, and with the Dodgers and Braves, Casey had inferior players. He was coming to a Yankee team that had Joe DiMaggio, Tommy Henrich, Phil Rizzuto, Yogi Berra, Hank Bauer, Gene Woodling and that great pitching staff of Vic Raschi, Allie Reynolds and Eddie Lopat, with Joe Page in the bullpen. It also was a team that had won a world championship in 1947 and finished a close third in 1948, just two and a half games behind Cleveland.

Still, there was a lot of doubt about Stengel's ability as a manager and a lot of pressure on Casey. But he managed the Yankees for twelve seasons and won ten pennants and seven world championships, including a record five straight world championships in his first five seasons. Casey was fired after the 1960 season, when we won the pennant and lost the World Series to the Pirates in that heartbreaker. He was seventy-one at the time and the Yankees felt he was too old to manage, so they replaced him with Ralph Houk.

The Mets brought Casey back to manage when they were formed in 1962, but it was mostly for publicity reasons. The team was lousy and Casey was seventy-three and starting to slow down. He managed the Mets for four years and might have continued, but he fell and broke his hip and didn't finish out the 1965 season.

Casey was pretty solid when I joined the Yankees in 1951. He was the boss, make no mistake about that, sixty years old or not. And I can tell you, I was in awe of him.

But Casey always liked me. He was always bragging on me during spring training that first year. He kept referring to me as "my boy." And I remember, in my first year, I was having a terrible time. I was only nineteen and still learning. I was striking out a lot, and not hitting much, and one day Casey called me into his office.

We were in Detroit and he let me get dressed and go out on the field for batting practice. He didn't want to cause a scene. He didn't want the other players to see me go into his office, because he had some bad news he had to deliver. He sent one of the coaches out to the field to tell me Casey wanted to see me in his office.

I guess I knew what was coming, and if I didn't, the look on Casey's face and the sound of his voice told me.

"I'm going to send you down to Kansas City," he started, and as he was talking, he was trying to fight back tears, but he couldn't. The next thing you know, Casey's crying and he's got me crying along with him.

"It's [sob] for your own [sob] good," he said. "You'll go down there and get your confidence back [sob] and you'll be back in six weeks [sob] and you'll be a better ballplayer when you come back."

"I know [sob]," I said.

The two of us had a good cry and I went down to Kansas City, but I was discouraged.

That was the lowest point of my career. I joined the Kansas City club in Columbus, Ohio, and the first time up I dragged a bunt for a base hit, which is something I did a lot later in my career. Whenever I was in a slump, I would drag a bunt for a base hit to snap myself out of the slump. So I did that my first time up in Kansas City and the manager, George Selkirk, who had replaced Babe Ruth in right field for the Yankees in 1935, talked to me the next inning.

"Mick," he said. "We know you can bunt. They didn't send you down here to learn how to bunt. They want you to swing the bat and start hitting the ball again and get your confidence back, then they'll bring you back up."

So I didn't bunt any more. He took that away from me and I was really pressing. I started thinking, "Maybe I can't play." I went 0 for 22 and we went back to Kansas City and that's when I called my dad in Oklahoma. I said, "Dad, I want you to come and get me. I can't play."

"Where you at?" he asked.

I told him I was at the LaSalle Hotel in Kansas City and he said he was on his way. He got in the car and drove all the way from Oklahoma to Kansas City, about 150 miles.

He got to the hotel and knocked on the door. I opened the door and he just walked in and the first thing he did was grab my suitcase, one of those old cardboard jobs. He slammed it on the bed and started throwing my clothes in it. And I'm just looking at him. He hasn't said a word.

"What are you doing?" I asked.

"I'm taking you home," he said, and I could see there was a tear in his eye. "You can work in the mines with me. I thought I raised a man. You're nothing but a coward. If you're going to give up on yourself, you might as well pack up and come home with me instead of wasting everybody's time."

I had expected him to pat me on the back and say, "Come on, Mick, hang in there, you can do it."

But he was packing to take me home. At least I thought he was, but he probably was using reverse psychology. Now I was begging him not to take me home, to let me stay. I finally persuaded him to let me stay. We sat up that night and we talked quite a bit and the next morning he went back to Oklahoma and I stayed.

That was the turning point in my career. I stayed and things turned around for me. I played forty games in Kansas City. I batted .361, hit 11 home runs and drove in 50 runs and the Yankees brought me back. When I rejoined the club, Casey told me, "I told you you'd be back."

As I look back on it, going down to Kansas City probably was the best thing I could have done. My confidence was shot and I needed to build it back up in the minor leagues. When I came back, I was much better prepared for big-league pitching. I also got a new number when I returned to the Yankees.

Pete Sheehy, our clubhouse manager, had given me number 6 that spring. It was his idea, he later told me, that I would follow the line of succession of Babe Ruth, who was number 3, Lou Gehrig, who was number 4, and Joe DiMaggio, who was number 5. And I would be number 6. While I was away, Bobby Brown had come back from the Army and Pete gave him number 6, so he gave me number 7. I've always been glad he did.

For Game 1 of the 1956 World Series, the starting pitchers were Sal Maglie for the Dodgers and Whitey for us. Casey decided to start with Whitey, even though the Dodgers were loaded with right-handed hitters and left-handers had a hard time winning in Ebbets Field. But Whitey was our ace, and on top of that he was our best clutch pitcher.

Maglie was an interesting story. He was one of those guys who jumped from the big leagues to the Mexican League after World War II, when a couple of rich Mexican brothers were raiding the major leagues, trying to form a league that would compete with ours. They offered a lot of money, so about ten or twelve guys jumped at it. Maglie was one. He had played only one season with the New York Giants and wasn't making a lot of money in the United States. He was getting a little older and he figured his days of making good money in the United States were numbered, so he took the Mexican League offer.

At the time, those players that jumped were banned by Commissioner Happy Chandler from returning to the major leagues. But the ban was lifted and Maglie returned to the Giants in 1950.

In Mexico, he learned a curveball that made him a much better pitcher. In his first three years back, he won 59 games and earned a reputation as one of the toughest guys on the mound. He was a fierce competitor who wouldn't think twice about knocking a hitter down. He liked to pitch up and in. He was a mean-looking guy on the mound. He always needed a shave. That plus the fact that he liked to "shave" hitters earned him the nickname "the Barber."

The Dodgers and their fans hated him because he beat them all the time and because he was always knocking their right-handed hitters down. The more the Dodgers complained, the more Maglie would knock them down. And the more he knocked them down, the tougher it was for them to hit him.

The Giants let Maglie go in 1955 and he came to the American League. He pitched a few games for the Cleveland Indians in 1955 and 1956, but we never did face him. Early in 1956, he was sold to the Dodgers. The guy they once hated in Brooklyn became a big favorite with Dodger fans. He was thirty-nine years old at the time, but he still knew how to pitch. And he still was a mean competitor. He won 13 games for the Dodgers in half a season and he even pitched a no-hitter. No question, the Dodgers would not have caught Milwaukee and won the pennant if not for Maglie. By the end of the season, he was their best pitcher, so he earned the starting assignment in the first game of the World Series.

President Eisenhower was going to throw out the first ball for the opening game. A few minutes before game time, all the players from both teams lined up along the foul line, the Dodgers along the first-base line, the Yankees along the third-base line. Then the huge gate in center field opened and several limousines entered the field from the street.

The last car was a convertible and the President rode in it. The car circled the field, the people cheering and Ike waving to them. Then the car stopped near home plate and the President got out and walked down both lines, shaking hands with every player and coach and both managers before throwing out the first ball. Then he was escorted to a box near the Dodgers' dugout by Ford Frick, the Commissioner of Baseball.

You know what usually happens when President Eisenhower attends a game. My good-luck charm was working again. Enos Slaughter, the second man to bat in the Series, singled and I followed with a home run to give us a 2–0 lead right away.

But Whitey didn't have it that day. He retired the Dodgers in order in the bottom of the first, but Jackie Robinson led off the second with a home run. Gil Hodges followed with a single and Carl Furillo doubled him home to tie the score, 2–2.

In the bottom of the third, Pee Wee Reese singled, Duke Snider followed with a single and after Robinson made out, Hodges hit a three-run homer and we were behind, 5–2.

Whitey was taken out for a pinch hitter in the fourth and Casey brought in Johnny Kucks to relieve him. That was a bit of a surprise, because everybody expected Kucks to start Game 2. He had been one of our most dependable pitchers all season, winning 18 games. He seemed the logical choice to be our pitcher in the second game and it seemed odd that Casey would bring him in when we were behind by three runs.

But it was early in the game and Stengel must have figured Kucks would hold them and we'd come from behind and win. It didn't work out that way.

Once he had a lead, Maglie was really tough. Billy knocked in a run with a single in the top of the fourth to make it 5–3, but the Dodgers scored in the bottom of the fourth on a single by Sandy Amoros. That guy again? That made it 6–3 and that's how it stayed. Maglie finished up the game for the win and we were down, one game to nothing.

The Dodgers were filled with confidence after winning the opener. They had beaten us the year before and they felt they could do it again. Beating our ace only increased their confidence.

The bus ride back to Manhattan wasn't much fun. And if there were a couple of hundred people lining the streets when we went to Brooklyn, when we left there must have been thousands of fans lining the street, yelling at us, cursing us and throwing things at our bus.

10

Mickey,
Willie and
the Duke

The next day, we made the bus trip to Brooklyn for Game 2 in a driving rain. It was raining so hard, it seemed unlikely we'd get the game in, and sure enough, after we spent several hours sitting around the tiny, cramped clubhouse, the game was called and rescheduled for the next day. We never even got to take batting practice.

The only good thing about the rain was that it meant there were no crowds lining the streets on our trip to and from Ebbets Field. But it cleared up the next day and the crowds were back, taunting us, jeering, shouting their obscenities, throwing things at our bus as we drove through the streets of Brooklyn to Ebbets Field for Game 2.

It was Friday, October 5, and the starting pitchers were Don Newcombe for them and Don Larsen for us. Newcombe was the Dodgers' ace. He had led the National League with 27 wins during the regular season. He was a hard-throwing right-hander who always gave me trouble. I just couldn't hit him to save myself. But the rest of our guys just seemed to feast on him, especially Yogi.

Newcombe had lost two games to the Yankees in the 1949 World Series, before I got there. He missed the 1952 and the 1953 Series because he was in the Army, but we beat him in his only start in the 1955 World Series, knocking him out in the sixth inning. So coming into this game, he was 0–3 in World Series games against the Yankees.

With Kucks used up in relief in Game 1, Casey went to Larsen as our starting pitcher for Game 2. Stengel had gambled by using Kucks in relief in Game 1 and lost, but we had confidence in Larsen. He had more experience than Kucks and he had had a pretty good season himself, winning 11 and losing 5. He had come to us the season before from the Baltimore Orioles in what may have been the biggest trade in baseball history. Biggest in the number of players involved, I mean.

It was made in two stages, and when it was completed, it involved eighteen players. We got Larsen, Bob Turley, Billy Hunter, a first baseman named Dick Kryhoski, Darrell Johnson, a catcher, and a couple of minor-leaguers named Jim Fridley and Mike Blyzka.

In return, we sent the Orioles pitchers Harry Byrd, Jim McDonald and Bill Miller, catchers Hal Smith (the same guy who would come back with the Pirates and hit the home run to tie us in the seventh game of the 1960 World Series), Don Leppert and Gus Triandos, infielders Kal Segrist and Willie Miranda, outfielders Ted Del Guercio and old favorite Gene Woodling, who was getting on in years, and a "player to be named later," pitcher Art Schallock, who we sent to Baltimore via waivers the next year. So we got seven players and we gave the Orioles eleven, practically a whole team, which they needed at the time. For us, the trade made our pitching staff.

We were looking for pitching and Turley and Larsen were the key players for us. Both were young and threw hard. Turley had won 14 and lost 15 in 1954 for the Orioles, not bad for a team that won only 54 games and lost 100. "Bullet Bob," as he was called, threw as hard as anybody in baseball at the time. His problem was finding home plate, but once he did, he became an outstanding pitcher. He won 17 games for us in 1955, but had some arm problems and slipped to 8–4 in 1956. Then he came back to win 13 games in 1957 and 21 games in 1958, the most in the American League and good enough to win the Cy Young Award.

In 1954, Larsen had a record of 3–21, but as Roger Craig once said, you have to be good to lose 20 games or else the manager won't keep sending you out there. He was 9–2 for us in 1955, pitching mostly as a spot starter and in relief. And he was 11–5 in 1956.

Don had adopted a no-windup delivery, which helped him become a better pitcher. Something about making his delivery more compact. You see a lot of pitchers doing it today, but back then it was considered kind of radical.

Ted Williams, who could hit anybody, once said that Larsen was the toughest pitcher he had to face because of the no-windup delivery. Williams felt he could time the pitcher off his windup, but with no windup, Larsen kept Williams off stride.

When he came to us, Larsen already had acquired something of a reputation as a hard drinker and a hell-raiser, even though he had been in the league only two years at the time. I must admit that none of it was exaggerated. Larsen was easily the greatest drinker I've known, and I've known some pretty good ones in my time.

But I was also surprised at the kind of guy he was. When you have the reputation Don had, people who don't know you think you're a difficult person and a guy who doesn't take too many things seriously. Nothing could have been further from the truth. Larsen was one of the most likable guys you'd ever want to meet. And while it's true that he liked his booze and he enjoyed his good times, he was all business when he was on the mound; one of the best competitors I've ever known.

Pretty soon the guys started calling him "Goony Bird" because of all the flaky things he would do. For example, Whitey tells a story about our trip to Japan after the 1955 season, the one which I left early. On the way to Japan, we stopped off for a few days in Hawaii, where we had to take shots. Billy and I refused to take the shots, but most of the guys did and the pitchers took their shots in their nonpitching arm because they hurt so much and there was a danger that their arm would swell up and they wouldn't be able to pitch.

One night, Whitey and his wife, Joan, went to dinner, then they toured some of the local watering holes. It was about 2 A.M. when they got back to the hotel, and just as they did, a cab pulled up and out stepped Larsen, weaving his way up the front steps of the Royal Hawaiian Hotel.

"Hey, Goony Bird," Whitey said. "How you doing?"

And Whitey said Larsen just looked at him and said, "You'd drink too if you got those shots."

Not that Larsen ever needed an excuse to drink. One time, during spring training, we all went out to see Frank Sinatra at a hotel in Miami Beach. Most of the guys went with their wives, but Don was single at the time and he went alone. As soon as we sat down, the first thing he did was order a beer. Then he had a rum and Coke. Then a scotch and soda. And he followed that with Canadian Club. I couldn't believe a guy would mix his drinks like that.

After a while, Larsen started hiccuping. He couldn't stop it. Finally, he asked the waiter to bring him a shot of vinegar. He slugged the vinegar down and the hiccups stopped. Just like that.

Another time we were in Boston at the end of the 1955 season. We needed one victory to clinch the pennant and Larsen was our starting pitcher. We were leading, 4–1, in the eighth inning when the Red Sox rallied. They put a few men on base and Casey went to the mound to get Larsen. He brought Whitey in to relieve him. Whitey got out of the jam and we won the game and clinched the pennant.

When we got to the clubhouse, we looked all around for Larsen. He was the winning pitcher of the pennant clincher and we wanted to congratulate him. But Goony was nowhere to be found. Somebody finally found him in a room next to the shower. He was sitting on a block of ice, still dressed in his uniform, drinking a beer. He was so nervous, Larsen said, he couldn't listen to the end of the game. So he grabbed a beer, then turned on all the showers to drown out the sound of the crowd and the radio that was playing in the clubhouse and he went into this little room. He sat down on a cake of ice and stuck his fingers in his ears so he wouldn't hear what happened in the game. He didn't know we had won until somebody went in the room and told him.

· · ·

Game 2 started and we jumped right on Newcombe to score a run in the first. Enos Slaughter singled with one out. Newcombe got me, but he walked Yogi and Joe Collins singled Slaughter home to give us a 1–0 lead. In the second, we got rid of Newcombe by scoring five runs. When I say "we," I mean the Yankees, not me, because I didn't contribute anything. But Billy started us off with an infield hit. After Jerry Coleman sacrificed Billy to second, Larsen, always a good hitter, knocked in a run with a single. Gil McDougald also singled. Slaughter hit into a force play and I followed with a walk, something I'm sure Newcombe didn't want to do. Not only did he always get me out, but walking me meant he had to face Yogi with the bases loaded. And Yogi just owned Newcombe.

As I said before, Ebbets Field was an easy park to hit home runs in, especially for a right-handed hitter. The distance to right field and right center wasn't far, but they had that 40-foot wall and screen in right, which made it tough to clear. Not for Yogi. He was a low-ball hitter and he liked to go down after a pitch and uppercut it, so Ebbets Field was made for him. Sure enough, Newcombe threw him a low fastball and Yogi golfed it over the screen for a grand slam. That was all for Newcombe and we had a 6–0 lead.

But Ebbets Field was a lot like Fenway Park in the sense that there's no such thing as a safe lead there. Especially with the Dodger hitters. Larsen had held the Dodgers scoreless in the first inning, even though he had trouble throwing strikes and walked two batters. But he got Jackie Robinson to hit a smash to Billy, who had started at third base, and Billy turned it into a double play to end the inning.

Things were different in the bottom of the second. Gil Hodges led off with a single and Sandy Amoros followed with a grounder to first baseman Collins that looked like another double play. But Joe dropped the ball as he was about to throw to second for an error that put Dodgers on first and second with none out.

Billy used to say that Collins had the shortest arms in baseball. When Billy made a bad throw, he'd get on Joe for not coming up with the ball and he'd go around mimicking him by pulling his arms up and shortening them by a few inches. It used to make Collins madder than hell.

Collins' error was a tough break for Goony because Collins was usually very good on ground balls. In fact, at the time he had played nineteen straight World Series games at first base without making an error.

Carl Furillo walked to load the bases and Roy Campanella knocked in a run with a sacrifice fly to Slaughter. Larsen got pinch hitter Dale Mitchell to foul out, but he walked Gilliam to load the bases again and Casey had seen enough. He brought in Kucks, who immediately served up a single to Pee Wee Reese for two runs. With Duke Snider coming up, Casey again went to the mound to try to stop the Dodgers right there. He brought in Tommy Byrne, a left-hander.

Snider had the reputation of not being able to hit left-handers. But that was early in his career. In 1956, he led the National League with 43 homers, so he was hitting everybody. And he got under a pitch from Byrne and drove it over the right-field screen for a three-run homer to tie the score, 6–6.

Snider was a terrific player and is now one of my favorite people. I didn't get to know him until the past few years when we kept running into each other at card shows and old-timers' games and I just think he's one hell of a guy. I enjoyed playing against him in those days. He was big and strong and he could hit the ball a ton. And he was an outstanding center fielder. He could run and he had a strong and accurate throwing arm.

· · ·

As I have mentioned, at that time there were a lot of arguments among fans in New York over who was the best center fielder in town—Willie Mays with the Giants, Snider of the Dodgers or me. The players never got involved in any of that, although I did try to check the box scores just to see how Willie and Duke were doing. Among the three of us, there's no doubt in my mind that Willie was the best. He hit 660 home runs and he was as great a fielder as there has ever been, or probably ever will be. He could do it all.

I respected Willie as much as any player I've ever played against. He was also a lot of fun to be around. I used to like to play golf with Willie. He was a hustler on the golf course, just like me, and whenever we played, we'd always be trying to outhustle one another, trying to get extra strokes.

That reminds me of a story that involved me and Willie and almost started a controversy over whether I was jealous of Mays.

The 1961 All-Star Game was played in Candlestick Park in San Francisco. Our last game before the All-Star Game was in Chicago and

Whitey and I decided that as long as we were halfway there, we would go out to San Francisco early and get in a little golf on Monday, a day off.

As soon as we got to town, Whitey called Toots Shor, who had come in from New York for the game, and asked him if he knew anyone who was a member of a golf club in San Francisco where we could get in a round. Toots called his friend Horace Stoneham, who owned the Giants, and Horace called us.

Horace arranged for his son Peter to pick us up at our hotel and drive us to his private golf club, the Olympic Club. We went out to the club, but we had nothing with us. No golf clubs, no shoes, nothing. So we went to the pro shop and rented clubs. Then we picked out shoes, golf gloves and sweaters, intending to pay for everything on the spot. But they wouldn't take cash, so we decided to sign Stoneham's name and settle up with him later. The bill came to about $400.

We finished our round, then went to the clubhouse for a few drinks, which we also charged to Stoneham. Then when we got back to the hotel, Whitey called Toots to get Stoneham's number. Toots said that wouldn't be necessary. He was having a cocktail party that night and Horace would be there. We could see him face-to-face.

We went to the party. Tony Martin, the singer, was there with his wife, Cyd Charisse. They were two of my all-time favorites. I used to see them in New York all the time. There were a few other celebrities at the party and Horace Stoneham. Whitey turns to me and says, "Give me $200."

I dig in my pocket for the $200 and give it to Whitey, who adds $200 of his own and goes over to Stoneham to tell him what we had done and pay him what we signed for.

"Hold it," Stoneham told Whitey. "I'll tell you what. If you get in the game tomorrow and you get Willie out, you don't owe me a thing. But if Willie gets a hit off you, then you owe me $800."

Whitey comes back and tells me about Stoneham's offer.

"Nothing doing," I said. "Willie kills you. You can't get him out. You don't have a chance. Just give him the $400."

Somehow, Whitey talked me into agreeing to the deal. His strongest argument was that he didn't think he'd even be pitching in the game. I bought it because I didn't think he'd pitch either, and all it would cost me was $200. But the next morning, when I picked up the newspaper, there it was in big, bold headlines: SPAHN AND FORD STARTING PITCHERS IN ALL-STAR GAME.

"There goes $400," I figured.

Whitey started the game and got the first two hitters out. Then Roberto Clemente doubled and that brought up Willie. I'm in center field and I'm as nervous as I've ever been in any game. More nervous than in the seventh game of the World Series. After all, I've got $400 riding on this at bat.

Whitey throws Willie a pitch and he hits a line drive just outside the left-field line, foul by inches. Strike one. Another pitch and Willie drives one deep to left, over the fence, over everything. Again, a foul ball. Strike two. Now I'm even more nervous. I figure, "The next pitch will cost me $400."

Even from center field, I could see what happened next. Whitey loaded one up and threw the damnedest spitter I've ever seen. The ball started out right at Willie's shoulder, coming straight at him. Willie thought it was going to hit him, so he bailed out, and all of a sudden the ball dipped and darted and sailed right over the plate.

I could hear umpire Ed Runge all the way out

in center field. "Strike three," he said. Music to my ears.

I came running in, clapping my hands and jumping up and down like it was the last out in the bottom of the ninth of the World Series. Willie saw me and couldn't understand what was going on. As he passed Whitey, Willie said, "What's that crazy bastard clapping for?"

"I'll tell you about it later," Whitey said.

A lot of fans and writers saw me clapping when Willie struck out and they naturally assumed it was because of some rivalry between us. That story got around and it was a little embarrassing. I was happy, not because Willie struck out, but because I had saved $400.

I made it a point to look for Willie after the game to explain why I was clapping after he struck out. I didn't want him to think that it was based on any rivalry between us or that I was happy because he looked bad. "Nothing personal," I told him. I told him the whole story about playing golf at Stoneham's club and charging everything to Horace and how he bet us double or nothing that Whitey couldn't get Willie out. When he heard the whole story, Willie started laughing like crazy with that high-pitched cackle of his.

Willie and I were, and still are, good friends. Even today, people ask me who was the best center fielder in New York in those days and I tell them how I feel. Just look at the bottom line. Lifetime, Willie was better than me or Duke.

Duke Snider's homer in Game 2 wiped out the last of our six-run lead and tied the score, but it was only the second inning. The Dodgers got another run in the bottom of the third and then Slaughter hit a sacrifice fly in the top of the fourth to tie it again, 7–7.

But then Gil Hodges hit a two-run double in the fourth and another two-run double in the fifth to make it 11–7. They scored two more in the eighth and we got one in the ninth and lost, 13–8.

We had blown a six-run lead *and* we had lost the first two games of the Series, which was beginning to look as bad as the 1955 Series.

The bus ride home from Brooklyn was what you might imagine. Thousands of fans lining the street, cursing us, throwing fruit and vegetables at the bus, clenching their fists. The Dodger fans were sky-high. They had us down, two games to nothing, and they were sure they were going to beat us for the second straight year.

We were down, no question about it, but we weren't beaten. At least we knew we would get them in our ballpark for the next three games.

11

Home
Sweet
Home

We wouldn't have won in 1956 without Johnny Kucks (*center*). This is the day he won his sixteenth game. Billy drove in our first three runs and I hit my forty-second homer.

This is a baseball. Not bad for a high school dropout, huh?

They made a big thing about the home run I hit off Chuck Stobbs in Washington, like giving me this 600-foot-long tape measure. Red Patterson, our director of public relations, said he measured it at 565 feet. To tell you the truth, I don't think he ever left the press box.

UPI

We ended a slump when we beat Kansas City, 9–3. I had four hits. Johnny Kucks was the winning pitcher. And Norm Siebern hit two home runs.

We were together a long time. Yogi was the best clutch hitter I ever saw . . . and I wouldn't want any other pitcher but my buddy Slick (Whitey Ford) pitching for me in a big game.

UPI/BETTMANN

After my father died, Casey Stengel was like a second father to me. Casey was always bragging on me. I wanted so much to live up to his predictions for me.

Billy and I were styling as we took off for a road trip. You can bet we did our share of partying on that trip.

Playing in the All-Star Game meant being a teammate, at least for a day, of Ted Williams, the greatest hitter I ever saw.

President Eisenhower attended the opening game of the 1956 World Series in Brooklyn. My good-luck charm. It seems whenever Ike showed up at a game, I hit a home run . . .

I hit one in my first at bat of the Series, against Sal Maglie in the first inning of Game 1. It came with Enos Slaughter (number 17) on base. Yogi (number 8) was the next hitter.

I didn't try to steal often because of my bad legs, but I took pride in my ability to steal a base when we needed it. This steal helped us score two runs in the fourth inning and beat the Dodgers, 6–2, to even the 1956 World Series at two games each.

I consider this the greatest catch I ever made. It certainly was the most important. It came against Gil Hodges in the fifth inning of Game 5 of the 1956 World Series and saved Don Larsen's perfect game. I think it would have been a home run in Brooklyn.

*Y*ou couldn't have overstated the importance of Game 3 of the Series. We were down, two games to nothing, and for the next three games we would be playing in Yankee Stadium, where we just had to win. We were also very confident playing at home. Our team was built for our ballpark, with good pitching, especially left-handed, and excellent defense and power from both sides of the plate.

The Dodgers, on the other hand, would be at

a great disadvantage in Yankee Stadium because their lineup and their power was almost exclusively right-handed, with the exception of Duke Snider.

We knew these three games at home were crucial, and we knew we had to sweep them. If we won just two out of three, that would mean we'd go back to Ebbets Field needing a sweep, which would be almost impossible. If we won fewer than two games at home, well, then it was all over. So we had to win the three middle games at Yankee Stadium, and we were confident that we could do it. We were realistic enough to know it wasn't going to be easy—they could get a great pitched game or one player could get hot and hit a couple of home runs to beat us—but we really thought we could sweep them at home. The Dodgers, of course, were just as confident that they could take one game at our place, so all they'd need was one out of two at their park to be world champions for the second straight year.

I woke up early on the morning of the third game. It was Saturday, October 6, a beautiful early autumn day in New York, clear and cool. I met up with Billy at the St. Moritz coffee shop for a quick cup of coffee. I never ate breakfast on the morning of a day game. I guess I was too nervous to eat. We decided to take a cab up to Yankee Stadium. Billy was especially quiet during the fifteen-minute cab ride to the Bronx, hardly saying a word. He was always an intense competitor, not only as a player but as a manager, playing cards, playing golf, anything he did. He hated to lose. He would do anything to win, and I mean *anything*.

You had to watch him all the time. When he was manager of the Yankees, he would go out to play golf with Gene Michael and Lou Piniella and they would catch him kicking the ball. They finally gave him a shoe with a pitcher's toe plate on it so he could kick the ball without ruining his shoe. When Billy played golf with them, Michael and Piniella used to call it "Billyball."

I know on the cab ride up to the Stadium, Billy was thinking about the Dodgers and how much he hated them. It killed Billy to think that they might beat us again and I know he was determined to do everything in his power not to let that happen.

We arrived at the Stadium at 10 A.M. for a two o'clock game. I liked to get to the ballpark early, to get into uniform and just hang around talking with the guys and getting my mind focused on the game ahead and the pitcher I was going to have to face. I liked to picture him in my mind, his delivery, his stuff, the speed of his fastball, the break and angle of his curve. If I had batted against him recently, I tried to remember how he got me out and what pitches I hit if I hit him.

But I didn't make a big deal out of it like some guys—Ted Williams, for example. I was never really a student of hitting. I just liked to have a mental picture of the guy I would be facing.

The Dodgers' starter for Game 3 was Roger Craig. I didn't know much about him. I couldn't even remember hitting against him before. I might have in an exhibition game, but that wouldn't help very much. Pitchers are often experimenting in the spring, not throwing their best stuff. Craig started the fifth game of the 1955 World Series and pitched six innings in a game the Dodgers won. But I sat out that game with my bad leg. So I would be hitting against Craig for the first time.

I could see him on the mound in my mind, a tall, lanky guy who seemed to be all arms and legs when he delivered the ball. His best pitch, I knew, was a sinker. He kept the ball down and he threw strikes, but he wasn't overpowering. Hell, I wasn't going to worry about him pitching against me. Let him worry about me hitting against him.

Casey decided to come back with Whitey, who would be pitching with only two days' rest but had only pitched three innings in the first game. I was glad Whitey was pitching for us, and it gave me confidence. I figured, "How often does Whitey have two bad games in a row?" Besides, my buddy never let us down in games we *had* to win. Of all the pitchers I have seen, he would be my choice to pitch a big game—and this one was about as big as they come.

It didn't matter that the Dodgers had so many right-handed power hitters. Whitey was a master at using the whole ballpark, getting those big hitters to hit the ball to the warning track in left center and center. And we had the extra advantage of having Whitey nullify Snider, their only left-handed power threat, in the short part of our ballpark.

There were more than seventy-three thousand in the ballpark that day—that was before Yankee Stadium was renovated and the capacity was reduced—and that alone was going to be a big lift for us, even though there were a lot of

Dodger fans in the crowd. That always happened when we played the Dodgers or Giants in the World Series, since we were all in the same city. Still, most of the seventy-three thousand fans in Yankee Stadium were rooting for the home team and that was going to help us—if we hit, pitched and fielded.

Whitey breezed through the first inning, getting Junior Gilliam on a ground ball to third and striking out Pee Wee Reese, another of my all-time favorite players, and Duke Snider. It was a good omen. Craig got the first two outs in the bottom of the first and I came up and decided to try a bunt. I managed to push it past the mound and beat it out for a base hit. I know some people will say it was wrong to bunt. I was the league's home-run leader and I should have been trying to hit one out to give us an early lead. But I just wanted to get something going, especially with Yogi up next. But Yogi grounded to second for the third out and that was that.

The Dodgers scored in the second. Jackie Robinson led off with a walk and Gil Hodges beat out an infield hit to deep short. It had the makings of a big inning, but then Bauer hauled down Carl Furillo's drive to deep right, on which Robinson tagged up and went to third, and Campanella flied to right too, deep enough to score Robinson after the catch. The Dodgers led 1–0, but we felt lucky to get out of the inning with only one run against us.

Leave it to Billy to get us even in the bottom of the second. With one out, he lined a home run into the seats in left field. Once again, Billy got a big hit in an important situation. Once again, he was the guy who fired us up. The guy was amazing. I'm convinced that he made himself better in clutch situations because he competed so intensely. If he could have maintained that intensity for a full season, he would have been a Hall of Fame player for sure.

Casey knew about Billy's intensity in the clutch, so he would always try to instigate something. If we went into a slump and lost three or four games in a row, Casey would tell him, "Billy, go out and start a fight."

Billy, for instance, always believed he could get under Don Newcombe's skin. Newcombe would be pitching against us and Billy would go out to the dugout when the Dodgers were taking batting practice and start yelling at Newcombe.

"You big bum," Billy would say. "You're not going to last past the third inning. You got no guts. We're the Yankees. You know you can't beat us."

Newcombe would just look at Billy and you

could almost see the steam coming out of his ears.

"You little runt," he would say. "I ought to come over there and pick you up and whip your ass."

"Oh yeah?" Billy would say. "When you put me down, I'll beat the shit out of you."

Nothing ever came of this. No fights or anything. But I always believed Billy got Newcombe so mad, it took away from his concentration, and that's one reason Newcombe never was able to beat us. Which, of course, was Billy's intention all along.

The score stayed 1–1 until the top of the sixth, when Reese hit a drive to deep left center. There was one out and I was playing Pee Wee at medium depth, trying to cut off the single, but he had surprising power for a guy his size and he drilled this ball. I took off after it but couldn't get to it, and Reese raced all the way to third. Against Snider, the next hitter, I played much deeper and he hit one right to me. There was no chance to get Reese, who tagged up after the catch. The Dodgers led, 2–1, and we had four innings to catch up.

Bauer started us off in the bottom of the sixth with a single. But Joe Collins flied to center and, with a chance to do some damage, I popped to

Hodges at first. Yogi picked me up with a single to right center, sending Hank to third. And then Enos Slaughter, that steady old veteran, drove one into the stands in right for a three-run homer to give us a 4–2 lead.

The Dodgers came fighting right back in the seventh. Hodges walked and Furillo hit one back to Whitey, the ball bouncing off his glove and ricocheting far enough away for Furillo to reach first and Hodges to go all the way to third. The Dodgers had the tying runs on with nobody out, and Casey got our bullpen up. He went out to the mound and I was hoping he would leave Whitey in there. He was the guy *I* wanted pitching with the game on the line. Casey must have read my thoughts, because after a brief visit with Whitey and Yogi, the Old Man turned and walked away, leaving Whitey in the game. I was confident my buddy would pitch us out of this jam.

He got the dangerous Roy Campanella to foul to Gil McDougald, who crossed the third-base line from his shortstop position to make the catch. The runners held at first and third. But then Charlie Neal bounced to Andy Carey at third and Andy bobbled the ball, so his throw home was too late to get Hodges. The score was 4–3 with runners on first and second and Randy

Jackson, a veteran right-handed power hitter, coming up to pinch-hit for Craig. Stengel stayed with Whitey, who got Jackson on a fly to left that might have been out of the ballpark in Ebbets Field. Once again, we were saved, and the Dodgers were frustrated, by Yankee Stadium. Junior Gilliam made the third out of the inning on a ground ball to shortstop, and we held our slim lead.

We added an insurance run in the eighth, thanks to an error by Neal with one out. Joe Collins was safe at first on Neal's throwing error and I came to bat with a chance to put the game away. I popped to second and I was so mad I wanted to smash my bat against the dugout wall. Good old Yogi picked me up with a double up the alley in right center to score Collins and we went into the ninth leading 5–3.

Carl Furillo led off the top of the ninth with a drive to the gap in right center. There was no chance for me or Hank to catch up with it. The ball hit the auxiliary scoreboard they used to have at the wall and took a crazy bounce toward right field. Hank, who played right field in Yankee Stadium like he designed it, came up with the carom as Furillo was racing for second. Then Furillo made a base running error.

I never like to criticize or second-guess an opponent, but I say this only because it's something young people should learn. It's one of the cardinal rules in baseball that you never make the first or the third out of an inning at third base. Why? Well, if you're on second base with none out, you can move around to score on two outs. And if you're on second base with two outs, you can score on a single. But if you're on third base with none out or two outs, it doesn't give you that much of an advantage. The idea is that if you try for third base with none out or two outs, you'd better be damn sure you're going to make it.

In this case, it made even less sense for Furillo to try for third because his team was down by two runs. His run meant nothing. It couldn't tie the score.

That's why I say Furillo used bad judgment trying to go to third, and Hank, who rarely made a mistake in right field, made a perfect recovery and throw to Billy, who made a perfect relay to Carey to get Furillo.

That took the heart out of the Dodgers. The next two hitters made out and we won, 5–3. We had won our first game of the Series, but we were only one third of the way to our goal—the crucial sweep of the three games at our ballpark. Still, we were feeling much better, more confident than ever. We thought we could win the next two games.

Billy and I shared a cab from Yankee Stadium back to the hotel and I could tell Billy was feeling a lot better about things. He even talked to me.

We parted company at the hotel. Billy went his way and I went mine. We didn't do much partying or staying out late during the World Series. For one thing, the games were too important. For another, all the games were played during the day and we had to be at the ballpark early. And for a third, and probably most important, Merlyn always came to the World Series from Dallas with our friends the Youngmans, and that sort of cramped my style. So we usually just had a leisurely dinner and turned in early.

12

*Getting
Even*

$\mathcal{B}$illy and I were not superstitious—well, maybe a little—but we still tried to follow the same routine for Game 4 that we did for Game 3. There was, however, one difference. This was a Sunday and Billy got up early and went to St. Patrick's Cathedral for mass.

That's something not too many people ever knew about Billy. For all the stories about his fights and his wild nightlife, Billy always attended mass on Sunday, home or away. Sometimes, he would even go on weekdays. In his own way, he was a very religious person. He spent the winter after the 1953 season living with me in Commerce, and every Sunday he would get up early, get in his car and drive more than thirty miles to Joplin, Missouri, to the nearest Catholic church so he could attend mass. And he would never eat meat on Fridays. When he started managing, he even began wearing a tiny gold cross on his cap.

By the time I woke up, Billy was back from mass and we were ready to head for the ballpark. Both of us always were early risers anyway, so we stopped in the St. Moritz coffee shop for a cup of coffee, then took a cab up to the Stadium. Billy was in a more talkative mood this time, talking about the game ahead. It amazed me, but even as a player Billy always talked about the game as if he was a manager. I don't think he was thinking about managing back then, it just was his approach to the game.

When we got to the Stadium, there was a different attitude in the clubhouse. Before Game 3, all the guys were kind of quiet. They weren't uptight or nervous, just very determined. Today, they seemed confident. There was a lot of talking and joking. Winning one game makes a big difference in the mood of the clubhouse. Even Frank Crosetti, our third-base coach, was laughing and joking. That was unusual. Crow had either played or coached in more World Series than anyone up to that time, but he was always very serious about the game.

The crowd was not as big as it had been for the third game. Still, it was just under seventy thousand and the fans were really into the game. I liked the noise, but that wasn't always the case. When I first came from Joplin to New York, big crowds used to scare the hell out of me.

Casey had named Tom Sturdivant as our starting pitcher for Game 4. Tom was in his first full season and he was one of our most dependable pitchers, finishing the regular season with a record of 16–8. He was a little mean on the mound, a great competitor who would knock a hitter down in a minute. He was used both as a starter and as a reliever. As a reliever, he was 6–2 with 5 saves. He started seventeen games and completed six of them, including two shutouts. And on top of that he was a pretty good hitter, batting .313 for the season.

Years later, when Sturdivant was pitching for Kansas City, I batted right-handed against him just for the fun of it. Tom promised not to throw me any curveballs. But his manager, another of my old teammates, Eddie Lopat, told Sturdivant to sidearm me and he struck me out. I batted right-handed against a right-handed pitcher only twice in my career. The first time was against Sturdivant. The second time was against Sandy Consuegra of the Washington Senators, who had a great screwball that always gave me trouble. Just like Sturdivant, he also sidearmed me and struck me out and that was the end of that experiment.

The Dodgers' starter was Carl Erskine, a veteran right-hander. Carl was a slim guy from Indiana, and even though he wasn't very big—about five-ten, 165 pounds—he could throw pretty hard and he had this great big overhand curveball that could give you fits. He had a record of 13–11, but I remembered Erskine well from the 1953 World Series. Boy, did I remember him!

We had won the first two games in Yankee Stadium, then went to Ebbets Field for Game 3. Erskine, who we knocked out in the first inning of Game 1, came back to pitch against Vic Raschi in the third game. And what a game it was, the Dodgers scoring a run in the bottom of the eighth to break a 2–2 tie and beat us, 3–2. Erskine was unbelievable that day. He had that overhand curveball working perfectly. The ball seemed, as they say, to be literally dropping off a table. It would come at you shoulder-high, then the next thing you knew, it would be at your knees, in the strike zone.

Erskine struck out 14 of us that day in 1953, a World Series record at the time. And I'm almost embarrassed to say that Carl struck me out *four* times that day. It was probably the worst day I ever had at the plate. Not that striking out was any novelty. I struck out 1,710 times in my career and led the league in strikeouts four times. When I retired, I was number one on the all-time list for strikeouts. I'm grateful guys like Reggie Jackson, Willie Stargell, Mike Schmidt, Tony Perez, Dave Kingman, Bobby Bonds and Lou Brock came along to take that record away from me.

The other thing I remember about that game Erskine pitched against us in the 1953 Series is Johnny Mize on our bench. Mize was this big guy from Georgia. "The Big Cat," they used to call him. He had had a great career in the National League with the St. Louis Cardinals and New York Giants. He had a lifetime batting average of .312 and 359 lifetime home runs, including 51 for the Giants in 1947. By the time the Yankees got him in 1949, he was thirty-six years old and finished as an everyday player. But he could still swing a bat and he became a very valuable player for us as a pinch hitter. He was, in fact, one of the best pinch hitters I ever saw.

Pinch hitting is a special art, something I personally could never be comfortable with. It takes great concentration and discipline, knowing you're only going to get one swing at a pitcher. You have to be patient and you have to have confidence and you have to be ready whenever the manager calls on you. John's experience, his ability to study pitchers and his great batting eye made him an ideal pinch hitter. Even in 1953, at the age of forty, John was dangerous.

John loved to talk. And he especially loved to talk about hitting. Now it's the 1953 World Series and he's watching Erskine mow us down with that big curveball, and Mize is sitting on the bench, talking a blue streak in that Georgia drawl of his, telling everybody around him how he used to hit Erskine when he was in the National League.

"Ain't that tough," Mize was saying. "Y'all just gotta move up in the box and hit that curveball before it breaks."

Finally, Mize got his chance in the ninth inning. Casey sent him up to pinch-hit for Raschi and what do you think John did? He struck out. On a curveball that bounced on the plate, just the thing he was warning everybody else against. Not only that, he was Erskine's fourteenth strikeout, the one that broke the World Series record. Some of the guys, especially Billy, couldn't help laughing at him. I even remember Billy saying, "Tell us again, John, how do you hit Erskine's curveball?"

So here was Erskine pitching Game 4 of the 1956 World Series with the Dodgers leading, two games to one. It wasn't the same Erskine we had faced in 1953, but he was still pretty tough. This time at least I hit the ball. In the bottom of the first, after Bauer flied out and Joe Collins doubled into the right-field corner, I grounded out to Gil Hodges at first. Yogi followed with a single and we took an early 1–0 lead.

Sturdivant held the Dodgers hitless until Snider led off the fourth with a double off the right-field wall. After Robinson fouled to Berra, Hodges lined a single over second to score Snider and tie the score, 1–1.

I started off the bottom of the fourth with a walk. I was running as Berra struck out and I made it safely into second ahead of Campanella's throw. The Dodgers decided to walk Enos Slaughter and pitch to Billy. Knowing Billy, you can bet that pissed him off and made him bear down even more and he came through with a single to left. I scored from second and Slaughter went to third. Gil McDougald knocked Enos in with a sacrifice fly to center and we had a 3–1 lead.

Erskine left for a pinch hitter in the top of the fifth. He was replaced by Ed Roebuck, another fastball, sinkerball pitcher, which I liked. I was a better low-ball hitter than I was a high-ball hitter. I led off the sixth with a shot into the bleachers in right center, my second homer of the Series, to give us a 4–1 lead.

In the bottom of the seventh, the Dodgers brought in a young pitcher I had never seen before. He was a big, tall right-hander, about six feet five, and he was an imposing figure on the mound. He could throw hard, but he was only twenty years old. His name was Don Drysdale.

This was Drysdale's rookie year. He would go on, of course, to be a great pitcher for the Dodgers in Los Angeles, winning more than 200 games in his career. And he would give me fits later on in the World Series of 1963. I'm glad I didn't have to face him more regularly than just in the World Series. I'm glad he was in the other league because I know he would have been tough for me, a high-fastball pitcher who liked to come in on you. That kind always gave me trouble, like Newcombe.

Drysdale was another of those guys, like Early Wynn and Sturdivant, who would knock you down as sure as look at you. I remember one time in spring training in Vero Beach, I bunted on him and beat it out for a hit. I was standing on first base and Don came over to me and said, "Don't ever do that again."

I said, "O.K.," and forgot about it.

The next time I faced him he hit me in the rump. There was a big black-and-blue mark where he had hit me and Don came over to our clubhouse after the game, saw the black-and-blue mark and said, "Do you want me to sign that for you?"

"Big D" is another of those guys that I've gotten to know since I've been out of baseball. I'll see him at golf tournaments and card shows and we've become good friends. A hell of a guy.

Well, Drysdale came in and Bauer hit a two-run homer off him in the seventh to make it 6–1. The Dodgers scored a run in the ninth on a double by Jackie Robinson and a single by Roy Campanella, but Sturdivant got the side out and we won, 6–2. Sturdivant had pitched a strong game, a six-hitter. We had evened the Series at two games apiece and our clubhouse was a pretty happy place. We felt we had the Dodgers where we wanted them, even though we still had a lot of work to do.

Word got around our clubhouse that Casey

had told Don Larsen he was going to be our starter for Game 5 the next day. That took most of us by surprise, because Goony Bird had been awful in Game 2, getting knocked out in the second inning. We thought it would be Bob Turley or Johnny Kucks. But who were we to question Stengel? I know I wasn't going to. If Casey thought Larsen was the right man to start, he must have had his reasons.

As we left the clubhouse that night, most of the guys went over to Goony Bird with one word of advice: "Make sure to get your rest."

Knowing Goony, I was sure that advice was going to fall on deaf ears.

13

Perfect

I've heard and read a lot of stories about how Don Larsen was out all night drinking and partying the night before he pitched Game 5 of the 1956 World Series. But I'm here to tell you that it's just not true. I know because I spent part of the night with him.

I'm not going to tell you Goony Bird was a Goody Two-Shoes. He loved to party and he could do it with the best of them. He liked to drink and he was a champion in that league too. But he also was one of the best competitors I have known. He liked his fun, but on the mound he was all business. There might have been times when he stayed up all night, drinking and partying, and pitched the next day, but he never would do that for such an important game as a World Series game. He just wouldn't let his teammates, and himself, down like that.

Larsen told me he was going to have dinner with some friends, then go over to Bill Taylor's saloon on West Fifty-seventh Street, across from the Henry Hudson Hotel, where Goony was living at the time. He asked me to join them there, and I did.

Taylor was a big, left-handed hitter from Alabama who was an outfielder with the New York Giants. He spent a little over three seasons with the Giants, then a season and a half with the Detroit Tigers before retiring. He wasn't much of a major-league player, but he was a good guy, and when he opened this saloon, a lot of players started hanging out there. It was one of Larsen's regular stops.

I caught up with Larsen and his friends about nine o'clock and I stayed there about an hour and a half. In that time, I didn't see Goony Bird have one drink. He was drinking ginger ale. And he was cold, stone sober.

I left Taylor's about ten-thirty and went back

to the St. Moritz. Later, I found out that Larsen left a few minutes after I did. He stopped for a pizza and took it back to his room at the Henry Hudson. One of Don's friends told me later that he saw Goony go upstairs to his room with his pizza. He was sober at the time and that's how he spent the night, unless he got smashed in his room, which I doubt. But, of course, it makes a better story to say Larsen was out all night the night before he pitched, partying and drinking and falling-down drunk. And because of his reputation, it was easy to believe those stories. It almost seemed that people wanted to believe them, as if that made what he did even more remarkable and dramatic.

Monday, October 8, was a beautiful autumn day in New York. The sun was shining brightly, the temperature was in the sixties and there were 64,519 fans in the big ballpark. A perfect day for baseball, and that's what it turned out to be for Larsen—a perfect day.

The Dodgers started the Barber, Sal Maglie, who had beaten us in the first game. So we knew we were going to have to get a good game from Goony Bird to beat Maglie and take the World

Series back to Brooklyn leading three games to two.

Right from the start, Larsen looked like he had his good stuff. He had adopted this no-windup delivery in which he didn't pump his arms or raise them over his head. He simply took the ball, brought his two hands to his midsection, pivoted and threw. It had helped him smooth out his delivery and improve his control. He had always had good stuff, but early on he suffered from a lack of control. Another thing about Larsen, he didn't waste time on the mound. Just took the ball, got the sign and pitched. As a fielder, let me tell you it's a pleasure to play behind a guy who does that. It keeps you on your toes.

That's the reason I used to love to play behind Whitey. He'd pitch a game in an hour and thirty minutes. Today, they're lucky to get it over in three hours and thirty minutes. With Whitey, who pitched fast and didn't walk too many hitters, you knew you had to stay alert in the field.

When a pitcher is all over the place, walking hitters and taking his sweet time between pitches, it makes his fielders relax and lose their concentration. You get restless and your mind wanders.

I used to think about my last at bat, or my

next at bat. Sometimes I might spot something nice in the stands, and I'd yell over to right field to Hank Bauer, "Hey, Hank, check that out about six rows back."

Sometimes, that lack of concentration could get you to mess up an important play. It happened to me a few times. I'd be showing Hank something in the stands and all of a sudden I'd hear *crack!* and I'd look to see where everybody's running.

Larsen retired the Dodgers quickly, and in order, in the first. He struck out Junior Gilliam, looking. Struck out Pee Wee Reese, looking. And got Duke Snider on a line drive to Bauer in right.

Maglie was even quicker in the bottom of the first. Bauer popped to short. Joe Collins tried a bunt and popped it to Jackie Robinson at third. And I lifted an easy fly to Sandy Amoros in left.

Robinson opened the Dodger second and I thought he had the first hit of the game. He hit a screaming line drive to third that caromed off Andy Carey's glove right to our shortstop, Gil McDougald, who was a great defensive player and very underrated. He played three positions —second, short and third—and played them well. We came up to the Yankees together, and we were rookies together in 1951. I was the one with the big buildup, but Gil was named American League Rookie of the Year. I got sent down to Kansas City, but Gil played in 131 games, splitting his time between second and third. He batted .306 and had 14 homers and 63 RBIs.

Gil had this real funny batting stance. He kind of held the bat almost parallel to the ground. Later, they changed his stance and got him to hold the bat straight up, but he still looked funny, kind of like a right-handed Stan Musial. But funny stance or not, Gil could hit. He wound up playing ten years with the Yankees, on eight pennant winners and five world champions, and he had a lifetime batting average of .276. He quit when he was only thirty-two. He could have kept playing, but he was slipping and he was too proud to play at less than his best.

In 1956, McDougald became our full-time shortstop after Phil Rizzuto was forced to retire, so he was at short when Robinson hit that smash off Carey's glove. Gil fielded it and quickly threw to first. Even though he was coming to the end of his career, Robinson still could run with that pigeon-toed style of his and McDougald's throw just beat him to first by half a step. Little did we know at the time how important that play was going to be.

After Robinson was thrown out, Gil Hodges

struck out and Amoros popped to Billy at second.

That's how it went for three innings. Neither side had a hit. Neither side had a base runner. Nine batters up, nine batters out for each team.

In the Dodger fourth, Gilliam and Reese both bounced to Billy and Snider threw a scare into us when he drilled a 2–0 pitch on a line into the lower deck in right field. But it curved foul. Larsen struck him out, looking. He had now gone four innings, twelve batters, without allowing a base runner.

In the bottom of the fourth, Maglie continued to match Larsen. Bauer grounded to third and Collins struck out and I was up for the second time. Maglie threw me a curveball that he got up a little more than he wanted and I hit it good. You always know when you've hit one. There's a special feeling when the bat makes contact with the ball. I knew I hit that one good and I knew I hit it far enough. It was just a question of staying fair. The ball just made it inside the right-field foul pole and into the seats. In the new Yankee Stadium, it probably would have hooked foul. But before they renovated the Stadium, it was only 296 feet down the line in right field and this one hooked just inside the pole. It landed in foul territory, but when it passed the pole it was fair. That was unusual for me. Most of my home runs were to left center, right center and dead center. I rarely pulled the ball. But anyway, with my home run we had our first hit off Maglie and we led, 1–0.

The turning point in the game, as far as Larsen was concerned, came in the top of the fifth. You could see the determination in Jackie Robinson's eyes as he led off the inning. And he hit a vicious drive deep to left field, but foul. Then he went the other way and drove it deep to right center, but Hank, who was a much better fielder than people gave him credit for, and had a great arm, had time to get back and haul it in for the first out.

Next, Gil Hodges was up. He, of course, was a big, strong guy who could hit the ball a mile. And he was a dead pull hitter, tailor-made for Ebbets Field, but frustrated so many times in Yankee Stadium. He would hit these tremendous shots to left center and center that would have been long gone in Brooklyn, but in Yankee Stadium they were just long outs.

In the 1952 World Series, Yankee Stadium just ate Hodges up. He must have hit at least a half dozen balls in our ballpark that would have been home runs in Brooklyn but were nothing more than long outs. He wound up 0 for 21 in

the World Series, a record. It got so bad, they tell
a story that during the World Series a priest saying Sunday mass in Brooklyn got up in the pulpit
and said, "It's too hot for a sermon today. Just
pray that Gil Hodges gets a hit."

But all the prayers in Brooklyn didn't help
him and Hodges failed to get a hit during the
entire 1952 Series.

Now he was batting with one out in the top
of the fifth and the Dodgers were still without a
hit. Because Hodges was so strong and such a
pull hitter, I backed up a few steps and moved
over a bit toward left field. It was a good thing I
did. The count went to 2–2 and Hodges grabbed
hold of a fastball and drove it on a line into left
center. It would have been in the seats in Ebbets
Field, but there was plenty of room to run in
Yankee Stadium and I ran like hell. I just put my
head down and took off as fast as I could. I
caught up with the ball as it was dropping, more
than four hundred feet from home plate. I had to
reach across my body to make the catch and
luckily the ball just plopped into my glove. If I'd
started a split second later, or been a step slower,
or if I hadn't shaded over on Hodges, the ball
would have dropped for at least a double. It was
the best catch I ever made. Some people might

question that, but there's certainly no question that it was the most *important* catch I ever made.

Sandy Amoros, the next batter, took a ball. Then a strike. Then he hit one into the right-field seats that went foul. Amoros then grounded to Billy at second. The Dodgers hit some shots off Larsen in that inning. Two foul home runs and Hodges' drive to deep left center. And still they had no hits. When things like that happen—the ball curving foul, hard shots hit right at fielders, balls caroming off the glove of one infielder to another—you begin to get the feeling that fate is on your side, and that the pitcher is going to pitch a no-hitter.

Up to that point, I had been in three no-hit games in my career. In 1951, Allie Reynolds pitched two of them for us. One in July at Cleveland and one in September against the Red Sox at Yankee Stadium. The next year, Virgil Trucks of the Tigers pitched a no-hitter against us at the Stadium. So I had some experience with no-hitters and I had the feeling Larsen was going to pitch one. Obviously, so did Goony Bird.

I came back to the dugout after the Dodgers batted and I was down by the water cooler getting a drink. And here comes Goony Bird over to me.

"Hey, Slick," he said. "Wouldn't it be funny if I pitched a no-hitter?"

"Get the hell out of here," I said.

I walked away from him to the other end of the dugout. It's one of baseball's oldest superstitions that you're not supposed to talk about a no-hitter. If you do, the superstition goes, you'll jinx the pitcher. But here was the pitcher talking about it himself. That's how loose he was. Some of the other guys told me he was up and down the bench all day talking about pitching a no-hitter and they all chased him away, or walked away from him, because they didn't want to be the one to jinx him, even if he didn't worry about jinxing himself.

The fans were really getting into it in the sixth inning, sensing that they were witnessing baseball history being made. They cheered every out. Every strike. And it wasn't only the fans who were getting excited. The players were too. I know I was.

Most people prefer high-scoring games, a lot of home runs. They're usually bored by low-run games. That goes for me too. But there's something special about a no-hitter that makes it more exciting than a 10–9 slugfest. As a fielder, you get turned on, your adrenaline is flowing and your concentration level is higher because you know one little mistake can cost your teammate his no-hitter. And you don't want to be the one to do that, especially in a World Series with a full house and millions listening on radio or watching on television.

Larsen continued mowing them down in the sixth. Carl Furillo hit a pop fly to short right that Billy went back for and caught on the outfield grass. Campanella also popped up. This time Billy ranged to short center for the catch.

The center fielder is supposed to be the quarterback of the outfield. He's the guy who has to call all fly balls and pop flies, and he has to take everything he can reach. But Billy was so intense, so hyper and so into the game that he was roaming all over the outfield for pop-ups that normally I would handle. After he made one catch in short center field, Billy said to me, "Hey, Mick, let me know when I'm getting close to the monuments."

There were two outs in the sixth inning, so Alston let Maglie bat. With nobody on base, there was no use sending up a pinch hitter. Besides, Maglie was pitching a terrific game and the Dodgers would still have three innings left. Maglie struck out. Six innings, still no base runner for the Dodgers.

Meanwhile, our thoughts were not so much

on Larsen's no-hitter, they were on winning the game. Maglie was pitching a great game himself and there was no guarantee our one-run lead was going to stand up. Andy Carey opened the bottom of the sixth with a line drive over Maglie's head for a single. Larsen sacrificed him to second and Bauer came through with a single to left to score Carey and make it 2–0. When Collins also singled, it meant I would be coming up with runners on first and third with one out and a chance to put the game away.

I hit the ball hard, but didn't get under it. It was a bullet to first, but Hodges, who was as good a defensive first baseman as I've ever seen, just scooped up the ball with those big hands of his and stepped on first for one out. Then he threw home to Campanella and they had Hank in a rundown. They finally tagged him out. We scored one run and led 2–0, but we'd wasted a great opportunity to put the game away and had to wonder if that would come back to haunt us. Needless to say, I was pissed that I let this opportunity pass me by.

Larsen was breezing now, as if the insurance run made him stronger and more confident. Gilliam hit the ball sharply, but right at McDougald to open the seventh inning. Reese hit a drive to deep center, but there was plenty of room for me to catch it. Snider, their most dangerous hitter in our ballpark, flied to left.

In the eighth, Robinson hit back to the mound. Hodges ran the count to 2–2, then hit a line drive right at Andy Carey at third. Amoros hit another one of those deep drives to center that I caught with plenty of room and that showed, once again, why they call center field and left field in Yankee Stadium "Death Valley."

Now it was the top of the ninth. Three more outs and baseball history would be made. Everybody in the ballpark knew Larsen had not given up a hit. You could hardly miss it. It was right there on the scoreboard for all to see. And even if the players were concentrating so hard that they didn't look at the scoreboard, we could hardly forget it because Larsen himself was telling us he had a no-hitter from the fifth inning on.

Even though I was aware of the no-hitter from about the fifth inning, it didn't occur to me until about the eighth that Goony Bird was pitching a perfect game. I began to think, "Hey, he hasn't pitched from a stretch all game." That meant nobody had reached base. No walks. No errors. Nothing.

In the history of baseball, there have been more than 200 no-hitters. But there have been only about a dozen perfect games. And, of course, there had never been a perfect game or a no-hitter pitched in the World Series.

The crowd was on its feet and I was so nervous I could feel my knees shaking. I played in more than 2,400 games in the major leagues, but I never was as nervous as I was in the ninth inning of that game, afraid I would do something to mess up Larsen's perfect game. If I dropped a fly ball, it wouldn't stop his no-hitter, but it would end his Perfect Game, and that added to my nervousness.

If there were any Dodger fans in Yankee Stadium that day, either you couldn't tell or they were rooting for Larsen and baseball history too.

Furillo fouled off two pitches, took a ball, fouled off two more, then flied to right. One out. Two to go.

Campanella fouled off the first pitch and the crowd roared. He hit the second pitch right at McDougald and the crowd roared again. McDougald pegged to Collins for the out and the crowd roared again, louder.

The Dodgers were down to their final out. It was Maglie's turn to bat, but Walter Alston sent up a pinch hitter, Dale Mitchell, a veteran left-handed hitter. I knew him well. He had spent a little over ten seasons with the Cleveland Indians and had a lifetime batting average of .312. He had very little power, only 41 home runs in eleven seasons, but he was a good contact hitter. He sprayed the ball all over the field and that made it impossible to defend against him.

Maglie had pitched a great game. He had allowed just five hits, three of them in one inning, but here he was on the short end of a 2–0 score and just one out away from being beaten by the greatest game ever pitched in the history of the World Series.

As Mitchell stepped in and went into his crouch, I shifted nervously in center field. "Please don't hit it to me," I kept thinking. Then: "Please hit it to me." I worried about him hitting a sinking line drive or a bloop that would fall in front of me. I worried where I should play him. "Should I come in a few steps? Go back? Should I move to my left a few steps? To my right?" I looked into the bench for help, as an outfielder usually does in this kind of situation, but nobody was looking at me. They were leaving it up to me. They didn't want to be responsible if I should mess up. So I just stayed right where I was.

The crowd was roaring and then there was a hush as Mitchell took a ball outside. Larsen went into his no-windup and fired a fastball for strike one. And the crowd roared again. Larsen got the ball, looked in for the sign and pitched. Strike two, swinging. Another huge roar from the crowd. One pitch away. Again Larsen delivered. Mitchell fouled it off and the crowd held its breath. From where I was standing, it looked like Mitchell was a little behind the ball with that last swing, so I took a chance and moved a few steps to my right and hoped he wouldn't hit it to my left, just a few steps out of my reach.

Now Larsen was ready again. He brought his hands to his midsection, pivoted and threw. Mitchell took a half swing, trying to hold up at the last instant. From that point on, everything was a blur. Umpire Babe Pinelli is pumping his right arm in the air, signaling strike three . . . Mitchell is arguing with Pinelli that he held up his swing in time . . . Yogi is bouncing out from behind the plate, dashing for the pitcher's mound and throwing himself into Larsen's arms with a leap and a dive like an Olympic high diver . . . the noise of the crowd is deafening . . . I'm running off the field and my teammates are running from all directions, heading toward the mound, some from the field, some from the bullpen, some from the dugout. It was pandemonium all the way into our clubhouse. Everybody is mobbing Larsen all the way, the players, some fans who got onto the field, the press trying to get to him for quotes.

It was a wild scene in our clubhouse. We took a long time getting out of there, partly because of the crowd, but mostly because we didn't want to leave. We had just been witnesses to, and participants in, the greatest game in World Series history. *Twenty-seven batters, twenty-seven outs.* Only 97 pitches. Two hours and six minutes. Seven strikeouts. And only once, to Pee Wee Reese, the second batter in the game, did Larsen so much as go to three balls on a batter.

Later Yogi told me that Larsen never shook him off once in the entire game. They were in perfect sync on every pitch. And, Yogi said, he never saw Larsen throw so hard or have such good control. "He hit every spot I wanted," Yogi said.

Here it is thirty-five years later and no pitcher has come close to pitching a no-hitter in the World Series.

In the New York *Daily News* the next day, Joe Trimble started his story: "The Imperfect Man pitched the Perfect Game yesterday . . ."

That says it all about Goony Bird and what he accomplished in Game 5 of that Series.

I have often wondered why Don Larsen, Goony Bird, was chosen to pitch the greatest game in baseball history. He wasn't a great pitcher. The 11 games he won for us in 1956 were the most he ever won in any season.

In December 1959, Larsen was traded to Kansas City in another multiplayer deal. The Yankees traded a lot with Kansas City in those days and this was another sad one for me. They had traded Billy Martin to Kansas City, remember? This time, they traded another good buddy of mine to Kansas City. Hank Bauer, the guy who had taken me under his wing, took me into his apartment, bought me a suit and showed me the ropes when I was a rookie. After playing with him for nine years, I was going to miss Hank.

But that was also the trade in which we acquired Roger Maris, who was going to become another of my good friends and who was going to help us win four more American League pennants.

Goony Bird, another good friend, went to Kansas City in that big trade, only three years after his perfect game. He hung around baseball for eight more seasons, even spending the 1966 season in the minor leagues, to try to get back to the majors. He eventually did, finishing up his career with the Chicago Cubs in 1967. He played with five major league teams after Kansas

City, never winning more than 8 games in one season and ending up with a career record of 81–91.

But for one day, he was the greatest pitcher in baseball history. Oddly, that never impressed him. He never capitalized on that game the way most other players would. Larsen had a strange attitude, an I-don't-care attitude. Not that he didn't care about winning. But if Mitchell had gotten a hit and spoiled his perfect game, and we had won anyway, Goony would have said, "The hell with it. Let's go have a beer."

14

Overtime

Don Larsen's perfect game dramatically changed the momentum of the 1956 World Series in our favor. We had swept the three games in Yankee Stadium to take a three-to-two lead, so we needed to win only one more game to reign as baseball's world champions for the first time since 1953. We were on an emotional high thanks to Goony Bird, and we were sure we would beat the Dodgers without having to go through the pressure of a seventh game.

Losing a perfect game, we thought, had to be

a crusher for any team, even one as good as the Dodgers. But this was the World Series and you don't quit after losing one game, no matter how devastating or embarrassing that loss might seem. It was, after all, just one loss.

The Dodgers were a veteran team, with plenty of confidence, pride and ego of their own. They had the mental discipline to put that one game behind them and concentrate on the game they were about to play. They still felt they could win the final two games at Ebbets Field and repeat as world champs. After all, they had won the first two games of the Series in their ballpark. And they had their loud, enthusiastic and sometimes half-crazy fans behind them—this old lady, Hilda Chester, with her cowbells and the Brooklyn Sym-Phoney Band, a group of off-key musicians who paraded through the stands playing their instruments and arousing the crowd and the players.

So while ordinarily you might expect a team that has just been no-hit to wilt, nobody thought the Dodgers were going to roll over and die.

We even had the pitching matchup in our favor for Game 6. We had Bob Turley, the hard-throwing right-hander, rested and ready. Like Larsen, Turley had adopted the no-windup delivery to cut down on wasted motion and improve his control. In the World Series, he'd pitched one scoreless inning in Game 1, and then in Game 2 Casey brought him in to face one man—Sandy Amoros—and he struck him out. He hadn't pitched since.

The Dodgers gambled and went with Clem Labine, who had primarily been a relief pitcher during the regular season. He had appeared in sixty-two games, fifty-nine of them in relief. He won 10 and led the National League with 19 saves. Out of three starts he'd completed one. In the World Series he had made only one appearance, pitching two innings in Game 3 and allowing one run. So you can see that Walter Alston was taking a big gamble by starting Labine.

Labine had a great overhand curveball that would start up around your shoulders and drop down around your knees. A lot like Carl Erskine's, and you know how tough he was for us to hit.

We figured that if we could stay close to him, eventually Labine would tire because he was not used to pitching nine innings, and then we'd get him. We figured wrong. But still Turley did a great job keeping us in the game.

Hank Bauer led off with a single, but was erased when Joe Collins hit into a double play.

Labine threw me that great curveball of his and I hit on top of it and rolled it weakly to second.

In our second inning, Yogi led off with a single and again Labine pitched out of any trouble.

Meanwhile, Turley was tough. Duke Snider got a single in the first with two outs and Hodges walked to lead off the second, but neither of them advanced.

We had a great opportunity to put the game away in the third. With two outs, Bauer got his second straight single and Collins beat out an infield hit. That put me up with two outs and two on, but the best I could do was a ground ball to Gil Hodges at first. I was so disgusted with myself, I think I threw my bat farther than I hit the ball.

The Dodgers got a break in the bottom of the third when, with one out, Enos Slaughter lost Junior Gilliam's fly ball in the sun and it fell for a hit. But Gilliam tried to stretch it into a double, and Enos recovered and threw to Billy for the out.

Billy got our fifth hit with two outs in the fourth, a line drive off the right-field wall that went for a single. In Yankee Stadium, it might have gone into the seats, but Ebbets Field had that high wall in right. And the Dodgers had

Carl Furillo, who learned to play that wall so well he knew every nook and cranny.

Turley breezed through the fourth—a strikeout, walk, fly ball to right, pop to third—and the fifth—striking out the side, Furillo, Campanella and Labine.

The game was still scoreless as we went to the sixth. Joe Collins led off and drove one to deep center, but Snider went back to make the catch just in front of the stands. It was a good sign. If Labine was getting tired, as we expected him to, it meant his curveball would be getting sluggish. He'd get it up and it would be easier to hit. But you couldn't prove that by me. For the third straight time, Labine threw me his curve and I beat it into the ground, to Gilliam at second. But Yogi came through with a double to right center and Slaughter drew a walk that might have been semi-intentional.

That brought up Billy with two outs and two runners on, another clutch situation. And, as I've said, Billy almost always came through in clutch situations. This time, though, he hit a foul pop to third and Robinson caught it for the third out.

Gilliam led off the bottom of the sixth with a walk. Turley had good stuff, but he was a little erratic with his control. The Dodgers weren't hitting him—only two hits through the first six innings, one of them a ball lost in the sun—but they were getting men on with walks. Gilliam's was the third. Reese, attempting to sacrifice, popped up his bunt and Yogi made the catch in foul territory. Snider followed with another walk, but then Turley got Robinson on a pop to Gil McDougald at short and Hodges on another pop to Billy at second.

You could really feel the tension as we went to the seventh, and you could hear the crowd buzzing. But we felt that most of the pressure was on the Dodgers. They had to win today. We still had tomorrow.

Both pitchers continued their mastery, retiring the side in order in the seventh. And we moved to the eighth, still scoreless.

Bauer struck out and Collins drilled one high and far to right field that would have been gone in Yankee Stadium. Again, that damned wall kept the ball in the ballpark. It hit off the scoreboard and Furillo played the carom perfectly to hold Collins to a double. With first base open, the Dodgers walked me intentionally, which I thought was crazy the way I was hitting (or not hitting) and the way Yogi was beating up on them. Shows what I know, and why I never would have made a good manager. I never would have walked me in that situation to pitch to Berra. But the Dodgers did and it paid off. Yogi flied out to Snider in center and Slaughter grounded to Gilliam at second.

Labine opened the bottom of the eighth with a drive into the left-field corner that bounced into the stands for a ground-rule double. It was only the third hit off Turley, but it was the second time in the last three innings the Dodgers put their leadoff man on base. Casey stayed with Turley, who reached back and struck out Gilliam, then got Reese to fly to me. Snider was intentionally walked to pitch to Robinson, who popped to Andy Carey at third. And we went to the ninth inning, the score still tied at 0–0 and the tension in the ballpark so thick you could almost see it.

We went out quickly in the top of the ninth. Three up, three down. Billy Martin, Gil McDougald, Andy Carey. None of them able to get the ball out of the infield. Clem Labine, the relief pitcher, the guy we thought would be lucky to last six innings, had shut us out for nine, under the most intense pressure you can imagine. There were about thirty-three thousand in Ebbets Field that day, but they sounded like a hundred thousand as the Dodgers came to bat against Turley in the bottom of the ninth, needing just one run to force a seventh game.

As tough as Labine had been on us, Turley was just as tough on them. It was remarkable, considering the tiny ballpark we were playing in and the caliber of hitters on each side, that neither team had scored as we went to the bottom of the ninth. There were seven players in that game who eventually made it to the Hall of Fame. The seven of us would hit almost two thousand home runs in our careers, and yet there was nothing but zeros up on the scoreboard in right center field.

Gil Hodges bounced back to the mound to open the bottom of the ninth. Turley walked Sandy Amoros. Carl Furillo and Roy Campanella both took shots at ending the game, but Slaughter caught Furillo's fly to left and I took in Campy's drive to center. And we went to the tenth inning.

Turley was our first batter in the top of the tenth. I was scheduled to bat fourth in the inning, meaning if any of the first three hitters got on, I would get another chance to hit. It was a chance I wanted badly.

I had not had a very good Series. I was coming off a terrific regular season and I had high hopes that I would just carry it through the World Series. I did hit three homers in the Series, and not many players have done that. One of those homers was the first run in Don Larsen's perfect game. But I left too many men on base to suit me; I let too many opportunities pass and I was pissed. I really wanted another chance in this game to get a big hit that would win the game, and the Series.

Casey let Turley bat to lead off the tenth, which may be surprising to some. But there was no reason to take him out of the game, the way he was pitching. He was still strong. Remember, too, that back then the game was different. We didn't have the great relief specialists that they have now, and pitchers back then were accustomed to going nine innings. More, if needed. Today, a pitcher goes six or seven and they get the bullpen up. They have middle-inning men and setup men and closers.

We had a good bullpen, not a great one. That is, no one guy like Joe Page or Sparky Lyle or Goose Gossage or Dennis Eckersley. Our strength was our starters and Turley was as good as anybody else we had, even after pitching nine innings.

Turley struck out. The next batter, Bauer, grounded to short. And Collins grounded to second for the third out, leaving me on deck. And the Dodgers came to bat in the bottom of the tenth.

All Casey wanted out of Turley was one more inning. He figured with the middle of our batting order coming up in the eleventh, we'd score at least one run. I was sure I would do something in my next time up—I was just hoping for the chance.

Labine was due to lead off the bottom of the tenth for the Dodgers and, like Stengel, Walter Alston let him bat. That meant Alston was prepared to send Labine out for the eleventh inning, if necessary.

Labine popped out to Billy Martin for the first out. But Gilliam walked and Reese sacrificed him to second. Alston was willing to take his chance with Snider, or with Jackie Robinson, in case Stengel decided to walk Duke. Which is exactly what Casey did. He wasn't going to be beaten by a left-handed hitter. It was the third time Snider was walked, the second straight time he was intentionally walked, and each time the strategy worked.

It should have worked again. Robinson hit a line drive directly at Slaughter in left that Enos could have caught standing right in his tracks. Instead, Slaughter misjudged the ball. I don't know if he lost it in the shadows, with the sun going down and dusk coming in, or if he simply didn't pick up the ball. That's the hardest ball for an outfielder, the one hit straight at him on a line. Whatever the reason, Slaughter took a couple of steps in and once he had committed himself, he was dead. The ball sailed over his head and went to the wall. Gilliam, running with two outs, scored easily from second and the Dodgers won the game, 1–0.

The crowd was going wild. I could feel my heart sink. Poor Turley. He had pitched a great game. He had allowed just four hits, and two of them were balls that Slaughter had misjudged, and he had nothing to show for it but an "L."

There was going to be a seventh game, and it was going to be in Ebbets Field, where we had played three times and lost them all. After losing on Don Larsen's perfect game, the Dodgers had come back to tie the Series, which meant they were going to be extra tough in Game 7, playing at home with the reversed momentum and all. They had to believe that fate was on their side.

Our clubhouse was like a morgue. Hardly anybody said a thing. Most guys just sat in front of their lockers with their heads in their hands, not moving for a long time. Occasionally, you would hear some guy blurt out a swear word, or somebody else throw a piece of his uniform on the floor, or somebody else begin to move slowly toward the shower.

I heard a sobbing noise and I looked over and saw Billy, his head in his hands and his body wracking with sobs. There were tears in his eyes. After a while, I saw him get up and walk into Stengel's office and I heard him talking to the Old Man.

Later, Billy told me what he had said to Stengel.

"Casey," Billy said, "you gotta get Moose [Skowron] and Ellie [Howard] in the game tomorrow. They can help. They can do the job. They're young and they're hungry. Give them a shot, you won't be sorry."

It was kind of nervy for Billy to be telling Stengel who to play. You just didn't do that in those days. A player never gave advice to a manager, least of all Stengel.

But that's the way Billy was, and Casey undoubtedly respected his opinion. He just said he'd think about it.

As bad as we felt losing to the Dodgers, the bus ride home was even worse. The Dodger fans lined the streets of Brooklyn for miles, it seemed, taunting us, throwing things at us, cursing us and promising they'd get us again tomorrow.

There was no response from any of the guys on the bus. No threats, no promises. But as my eyes roamed around, I could see the look of determination in a lot of eyes on that bus.

15

Champs Again

$\mathcal{B}$illy was in a particularly sour mood on the morning of the seventh game. I mean, this time he wasn't talking at all. He was mad. He was still burning over losing Game 6. Not just losing it, but the way we lost it, on a ball that should have been caught being misjudged by an outfielder. As a player or a manager, Billy never could stand to see a player make a mistake.

He was approaching Game 7 like it was war, and I was glad. I knew that meant Billy was going to have a good game.

We had our morning coffee, then walked over to the Yankees' office to meet the bus for the long ride to Brooklyn. We knew what to expect on the ride over, and we weren't disappointed. They were out in force, the Dodger fans lining the street with their signs and posters and their curses and shouts. If it was any consolation, at least we knew this was going to be the last time we would have to take that bus ride this year.

Whatever Billy had said to Casey after the sixth game must have registered with the Old Man. Either that or Stengel was thinking the same as Billy. Or maybe he was just playing a hunch. Stengel often did that, and more often than not, his hunches paid off. Whatever the reason, Casey had shaken up his lineup.

He moved Billy up to bat second behind Bauer. Stengel must have figured, as I did, that Billy was so pissed off, he was going to have a big game. As Billy suggested, Moose Skowron was at first base in place of Joe Collins and Elston Howard was in left field in place of Enos Slaughter, who had misjudged two balls the day before, including the one that cost us the game. Moose was hitting fifth behind me and Yogi. Ellie batted sixth. Then came Gil McDougald and

Andy Carey. To pitch this critical game, Casey had chosen Johnny Kucks.

Kucks was a local guy, from Hoboken, New Jersey, who grew up rooting for the Yankees and got to fulfill any kid's dream by playing for his favorite team. His regular season record was 18–9, second only to Whitey. He was the logical guy to start this important game, although we would rather have had Whitey, because he was so tough in big games and Kucks was in only his second year in the big leagues.

Whitey had pitched Game 3 in Yankee Stadium and won without too much trouble. He could easily have come back in Game 7. He would have been pitching with three days' rest which was sufficient. But I guess Stengel wanted a right-handed pitcher in Ebbets Field, with all those right-handed power hitters in that little ballpark. And besides, Whitey would be in the bullpen in case Kucks got into trouble early.

What made Casey's decision to start Kucks in the big game so surprising was that Johnny had not started a game in the Series. He'd pitched two innings in relief in Game 1 and he faced one batter in Game 2 and gave up a two-run single. And he hadn't pitched since. At least he was well rested.

The other surprising move was Stengel playing Skowron and Howard, both right-handed batters and both relatively inexperienced, in place of Collins and Slaughter, two veteran left-handed hitters. The Dodgers were starting Don Newcombe, a right-hander, so you might have expected Casey to stack his lineup with left-handed hitters. He went just the opposite. He started only two left-handed hitters, me and Yogi. And I didn't count. As I said before, I never could hit Newcombe.

I was not having a very good Series for a Triple Crown winner. Coming into the final game, I was batting .250 on five hits in twenty at bats. True, three of my hits were homers and I knocked in four runs, but I felt I should have done better. If I had, we might not be playing a seventh game.

Even with my nemesis, Newcombe, pitching against us, I wasn't worried. The other guys, especially Yogi, just wore him out. Newcombe had started Game 2 and we—meaning my teammates —knocked him out in the second, scoring five runs, four of them on Yogi's grand slam.

As I said, Howard and Skowron both were inexperienced. Ellie had come up in 1955, and although he was going to become a great player, and Yogi's successor as our catcher, he wasn't there yet. He batted .290 and .262 and had a total of 15 homers and 77 RBIs for his first two seasons. What's more, he hadn't played at all in the first six games of the Series, not even as a pinch hitter. But I guess Casey knew what he was doing. At least I hoped he did.

Of all the Yankees I played with, I probably go back farther with Moose Skowron than any of my other teammates. I first met Moose late in the 1950 season. I wasn't even nineteen years old and I had just finished my second season of pro ball with Joplin, a Class A club. I had had a pretty good year—a .383 batting average, 26 homers, 136 RBIs—so the Yankees brought me up after my season was over to take a look at me and kind of get me accustomed to being around a big-league team. I joined them in St. Louis, then we went on to Chicago, which is where I first met Moose.

He was from Chicago and he was just eighteen years old. He had played football at Purdue. A pretty good punter, I've been told. He had just signed a contract with the Yankees, and although he hadn't played any pro ball at that time, they wanted to take a look at him too. There was a third kid, an infielder named Kal Segrist, who was from Texas and was one of the first bonus babies in baseball. The Yankees gave him a $50,000 bonus to sign, which sounded like all the money in the world to me at the time. They gave him $50,000 and Segrist played only two years in the big leagues. I got $500 to sign and I played eighteen seasons.

Since Moose and I were a couple of kids, they roomed us together. One thing I remember about Moose—and I don't know why I remember this after all these years—he had bad feet. It looked like his toes were rotted off. The other thing I remember is how strong he was. He could really hit.

We would work out with the Yankees before the game and they would watch us field and watch us hit and the coaches would help us correct our mistakes if they saw something we were doing wrong. We would take batting practice with the extra men. We wouldn't hit against the front-line pitchers, like Raschi, Reynolds, Lopat and Ford. We'd hit against the second-line pitchers and they wouldn't tell us what was coming. I was impressed with how far Moose hit the ball. He had great power.

Lew Burdette was with the Yankees then before he was traded to the Braves, and he was just as mean then as he was later. He wouldn't give you anything to hit, not even in batting practice, and here we were two kids, trying to impress Casey, and the coaches and Burdette was bearing down, trying to make us look bad. And he did. We couldn't even foul one in the cage. That really got us mad and I remember Moose hitting a three-run homer off Burdette in the 1958 World Series, and as he rounded third, he shouted out to the mound, "That makes up for 1950."

We left Chicago and went to New York, where we would stay for a week so we could get a lot of instruction and the Yankees could get a real good look at us. Moose and I roomed together at the Concourse Plaza in the Bronx, right up the hill from Yankee Stadium, within walking distance of the park. That's when I got to know him better, although both of us were quiet in those days.

One time we went downtown to Manhattan to buy gifts for our girlfriends. We were walking along Broadway and there was a guy in a storefront twirling some dough up in the air and Moose said, "Hey, Mick, let's get a slice of pizza."

To tell you the truth, I had never had pizza before. I didn't even know what it was. But Moose did. Coming from Chicago, he ate pizza all the time. And he loved it. So we stopped in the store and he ordered two slices, one for him and one for me, and that was the first time I ever ate pizza. But not the last, I can assure you.

When our week was over, the Yankees gave us airplane tickets. I was going home to Oklahoma and Moose was going to Puerto Rico to play winter ball. Frank Scott, the team's traveling secretary, asked us how much we spent during the week. We didn't spend much. We ate most of our meals in the hotel and signed for them and we didn't go out a lot. Besides, everything was much cheaper back then.

So Moose tells Frank we spent about $20 or $30 each.

"That's all you spent?" Scott said. "You're in the big leagues now. This is the Yankees."

And he gave us each a check for $100.

It wasn't until four years later that Moose came up to the Yankees after three good years in the minor leagues. In 1952, his second year in pro ball, he played for Kansas City in the American Association and batted .341 and led the league with 31 home runs and 134 RBIs. Believe it or not, after a year like that in class Triple A, they still sent him back in 1953, and he batted .318 with 15 homers and 89 RBIs. So he came up in 1954, but he played in only 87 games because we had Joe Collins at first. Moose batted .340, and little by little, over the next two years, he was playing more and more.

In 1955, he played in 108 games and batted

.319 with 12 homers and 61 RBIs. In 1956, he played in 134 games and batted .308 with 23 homers and 90 RBIs. He was quickly becoming one of the best hitters in the American League.

Moose is one of the meanest-looking guys you'll ever want to see, but he's also one of the gentlest, sweetest people you'll ever meet. Oh, he can be tough if you cross him, but usually he's kind and easygoing.

He used to have the locker between me and Yogi, and one time, during spring training, I asked him, "Moose, don't you like me? How come you never want to go out with me?"

He just shrugged and said it was nothing personal, but he just didn't live the kind of lifestyle we did. But we kept begging him and one day he agreed to come out. It was the spring of 1961. Ralph Houk was the manager and Whitey and I set it up. We went to Ralph and told him we wanted to take Moose out for one night. Houk agreed to go along with the gag.

So we rented a limousine and we picked Moose up and handed him a chauffeur's cap and told him he was to be our chauffeur. Moose played along with us. We sat in the back of the car and he drove us around, wearing his little cap. We'd tell him where we wanted to go and we'd pull up to the place and tell Moose to go in and tell the manager who he had in the car. And he did. And the manager would come out, and see us, and invite us in. We'd have a few drinks, then we'd go on to another place.

This went on all night. We got so smashed, Moose included, that we went bowling at four o'clock in the morning. We didn't get home until after 6 A.M. and we had a game in Clearwater that day.

We finally got to the park and I could tell Moose was struggling. But we set it up with Houk and he put Moose's name in the lineup. I thought he was going to die right there while he was taking infield.

"Mick," he said, "I can't play."

"You got to, Moose," I said. "You can't tell Houk you were out all night. He'll go crazy and he'll fine you. You got to get through it."

And of course we had it all set up with Houk, and when the game started, Houk took Moose out of the lineup and the three of us sat alongside the fence for the game. And that was the last time he ever went out with us, although we were close friends and we remain close friends to this day.

• • •

Skowron had started the first game of the 1956 World Series and went 0 for 4 against Sal Maglie. That's when Stengel switched to Joe Collins, a more experienced player and a left-handed hitter, in Game 2. Joe got a couple of hits and we won Game 3, so Casey just stayed with him, and Moose stayed on the bench. He pinch-hit in the second game and made out and didn't get into Games 3, 4, 5 and 6 at all. So, coming into the seventh game, Skowron was 0 for 5 for the Series, and it surprised a lot of people that Moose started and batted fifth. To this day, Moose believes it was Billy who got him in the game.

Bauer led off with a sharp single to left off Newcombe. But Newk was really throwing and he struck out Billy and me with hard stuff. That brought up Yogi, who loved hard stuff and, as I said, always hit Newcombe well. Newcombe made the mistake of getting one up in Yogi's eyes and Yogi drove it over the screen in right field and, just like that, we had a 2–0 lead.

It stayed like that going into the third. Kucks was pitching well in the early innings. He survived a walk and a single with one out in the first by getting Jackie Robinson to hit into a double play. And in the second he got three ground balls with his good sinker.

Hank tried to beat out a bunt to start the

third and was thrown out. But Billy lined a single to center. For the second straight time, Newcombe struck me out, and Yogi came to bat with one on and two outs, just like in the first inning. Yogi got a break when he foul-tipped a third strike and Campanella couldn't hold it. Yogi had another life. This time he hit one even farther than the first time, driving it over the scoreboard in right center for his second straight two-run homer. In the Series, Yogi had batted against Newcombe three times and hit three home runs good for eight RBIs.

Newcombe was allowed to finish the inning, but when Ellie Howard led off the fourth with a drive over the scoreboard, that was all for Newcombe. We didn't know it at the time, but after he came out of the game, Newcombe dressed quickly and left. Immediately outside the ballpark, he got involved in an altercation with a parking-lot attendant. The attendant apparently had made some remark to Newk, something about his lack of courage, and Newcombe just came apart. He hauled off and slugged the guy. The parking-lot attendant sued Newcombe. They settled out of court, but Newcombe never was the same after that.

He had won 27 games in 1956, the most in baseball. The following year, he won just 11.

The year after that, he was traded to Cincinnati. He no longer was the dominant pitcher he had been. He wound up going to play in Japan and later he admitted he had a drinking problem and checked himself into a rehab clinic before it became fashionable to do so. A lot of people attributed Newcombe's problems to what happened to him in that seventh game, but that's an easy cop-out. To his credit, Newcombe never used that as an excuse for his problems. Also to his credit, he straightened himself out and turned his life around. Today, he works with the Los Angeles Dodgers as a counselor against drugs and alcohol. I still see him from time to time. I always liked Newk—except when he was on the mound.

With a 5–0 lead and Kucks pitching so well, throwing his sinker and getting the Dodgers to hit the ball on the ground, we felt pretty good about things. Besides, we still had Whitey in the bullpen in case Kucks got into trouble.

It's always interesting when you take control of a game, especially such a big game, in the other team's ballpark. It's as if you're playing to an empty stadium, it's so quiet. Occasionally, the Dodger fans would try to rally their team with applause, but it was hopeless.

With Newcombe out of the game, I managed to get a hit—a double off Don Bessent in the fifth, but nothing came of it. Then in the seventh, we put the game away with Roger Craig pitching for the Dodgers. Billy singled to left and I followed with a walk. A wild pitch moved us up to second and third and, with first base open, the Dodgers walked Yogi intentionally. They had seen enough of him for one day.

That meant Moose was batting with the bases loaded and he lined one into the left-field seats. It was his only hit of the Series, but it accounted for four runs. I was really happy for him. I couldn't have been happier if I'd hit that ball myself.

We had a 9–0 lead and from then on, it was all anticlimactic, only a matter of time before the Dodgers would go down, which they did. Kucks finished up and completed his shutout. With two outs in the bottom of the ninth, Jackie Robinson struck out. Yogi dropped the ball, but picked it up quickly and threw to Moose at first and we were world champions again.

Ironically, that strikeout by Jackie Robinson was his last at bat in the major leagues. After the season, the Dodgers traded him to the hated Giants, but Jackie refused to report to the Giants and retired instead. He took a job as an executive with the Chock Full O' Nuts coffee company.

That game was also the last World Series game ever played in Ebbets Field. The following year, the Dodgers finished in third place, behind the Milwaukee Braves and the St. Louis Cardinals. In 1958, the Dodgers left Brooklyn and moved to Los Angeles. About a year or two later, Ebbets Field was torn down and a housing project was built in its place.

It's interesting that Skowron and Howard, the two men Stengel gambled on, the two guys who Billy talked into the lineup, each contributed a home run and knocked in five runs between them. But the real heroes of the game for us were Yogi, with his two homers off Newcombe and four runs batted in, and Kucks, who shut the Dodgers down on three hits, two singles by Duke Snider and one by Carl Furillo. When you can shut out a great-hitting team like the Dodgers, and do it in their ballpark, you have accomplished something.

Yogi not only had a great game, he had a great Series. He easily would have been the hero of the World Series. It took a perfect game, something never done before in World Series history, for him not to be named Most Valuable Player of the Series.

Yogi batted .360 on nine hits in twenty-five at bats. He hit three home runs and knocked in ten runs. Enos Slaughter batted .350 and he, Moose and I each knocked in four runs, second to Yogi. Billy had his usual good Series with a .296 average and three runs batted in. Yogi and I tied for the lead in home runs with three.

For the Dodgers, Gil Hodges and Duke Snider each batted .304. Gil knocked in eight runs and Duke four, and each hit one homer. No Dodger hit more than one. And no pitcher on either team won more than one game or lost more than one.

Our clubhouse was a happy one, but it wasn't wild, probably because the game had been a blowout. It never really was in doubt after Yogi's second homer KO'd Newcombe in the third. The Yankees were world champions once again and that's what really mattered.

The best part was the bus ride home, through the streets of Brooklyn. There were no fans lining the streets on our route to Manhattan. No shouts, no curses, no threats. Nothing. Just our championship bus rolling along, carrying a bunch of noisy and happy players. World champions!

EPILOGUE

If I could do anything over again from the 1956 season, I would like to have a better World Series. I batted only .250. I did hit three homers, but I only drove in four runs. I've had much better World Series.

But the Yankees won and that's the main thing. Except for that disappointing World Series performance, 1956 was a great year, the best I ever had in baseball. I would never again duplicate that season, and I played until 1968. I established myself in 1956, I finally accomplished the things people had been predicting for me, especially Casey Stengel, and I felt good about that.

I was also named Most Valuable Player in the American League, my first of three MVP awards. I would win it again in 1957 and 1962.

The Most Valuable Player in the National League was Don Newcombe for his 27 victories. It should be pointed out that votes for MVP, cast by a committee made up of members of the Baseball Writers Association, must be in before the start of postseason play. So the MVP award does not take into account anything that happens after the final game of the season. A good World Series doesn't help, a bad World Series doesn't hurt.

Newcombe also won the Cy Young Award. Back then, they gave only one Cy Young. It wasn't until eleven years later that they began awarding one in each league. Luis Aparicio of the Chicago White Sox was the American League Rookie of the Year in 1956. Frank Robinson, then with the Cincinnati Reds, was the National League Rookie of the Year.

I made $32,500 in 1956, and after my big year, I expected a big raise and I got it. The Yankees doubled my salary to $65,000, a staggering amount in those days.

We didn't have agents back then. There were

no agents. Besides, if any Yankee had walked into George Weiss's office with an agent to talk contract, Weiss would have thrown the player, and the agent, out on their ass. We had a union, but it didn't have the clout it got once Marvin Miller came in to run it.

I never was much for unions in baseball anyway. I never sat in on any of their meetings. I didn't like the idea of baseball players having a union, although I guess it's necessary for some people. But I was opposed to walkouts and strikes and all the things a union needs to get what it wants. I just wanted to play baseball.

In my day, baseball players had very few rights and very little leverage. We pretty much played for the amount the club dictated. We did our own salary negotiations and most of us weren't sophisticated enough or courageous enough or experienced enough at negotiations to squeeze the club for more money. Often, how much you were paid had less to do with how much you produced than it did with how good you were at negotiating.

Moose Skowron, for example, always was underpaid because he hated to haggle over money. The club named a figure and Moose might ask for a little more, but he'd never hold them up. He usually accepted their offer. Yogi, on the other hand, was smart. He'd wait until after we'd won the World Series and we were at our victory party. Then he'd seek out Del Webb or Dan Topping, the co-owners of the Yankees, and talk contract for the following year. That was another thing. There was no such thing as multiyear contracts in those days. Anyway, Yogi would find Topping and Webb at the victory party and they'd be in a good mood because we had just won a world championship, and maybe they'd be in the sauce a little, or more than a little, and Yogi would tell them what he wanted, which usually was more than George Weiss would want to pay him.

"O.K.," Topping would say. "You got it. Come in tomorrow or the next day and we'll have the contract drawn up and you can sign it."

That used to make Weiss mad, because he never would have agreed to what Topping and Webb gave Yogi. But what could he do? They were the bosses. And that's how Yogi, dumb like a fox Yogi, always got a good contract.

In 1957, I won my second consecutive Most Valuable Player award. My average went from .353 to .365, but I didn't win the batting title. Ted Williams, at age thirty-nine, batted an unbelievable .388.

My home runs fell off from 52 to 34 and my

RBIs from 130 to 94. Why? you wonder. Well, let's face it, to hit 52 homers and drive in 130 runs, everything has to go right for you, which it did for me in 1956. The following year, I had a few more injuries. I missed ten games and I had about seventy fewer at bats than the year before. And I just wasn't getting as many good pitches to hit. My walks went from 112 in 1956 to 146 in 1957.

Still, I thought I had a pretty good year. Good enough to win the MVP, as I said, and good enough, I figured, to earn a raise. But after that season, Weiss sent me a contract calling for a $10,000 cut. I couldn't believe it. When I asked him about it, he said I deserved the cut because I didn't have as good a year as in 1956. I wound up signing for $75,000, a $10,000 raise, and that was because Del Webb and Dan Topping stepped in and told Weiss to give it to me.

One time, I held out and didn't report to spring training because I was unhappy with the contract Weiss sent me. Weiss called me and said if I didn't report, he was going to trade me to Cleveland for Rocky Colavito and Herb Score. Cleveland? I was in spring training the next day.

I eventually got up to $100,000, but that's as high as I got. For the last six years of my career, I got the same contract, an automatic $100,000, which was kind of an unwritten maximum in baseball back then. Hell, in the last three years of my career, I didn't deserve a raise. I was more than happy with my contract. I always thought I was being overpaid at $100,000.

Another thing I don't like besides walkouts and strikes and all, is long-term contracts for players. I'm convinced that for most players it takes away their incentive to have a good year. They have their money, so what's the motivation to have a good year? They're going to get the same money next year no matter what kind of season they have. That's not true of all players, but I think it's true of a lot of them, even if it's only subconscious.

The disabled list is another thing that has become a big thing today. You see guys going on the disabled list all the time. Why? It doesn't matter if they don't produce; they have their long-term contracts. Back in my time, if you didn't produce, you didn't get a raise, so players played hurt because you can't put up numbers when you're on the disabled list. I'm not saying you should play hurt, but neither should you be on the DL every other week. Anyway, that's why I always believed in a one-year contract. It made you put out and produce. Produce this year and get rewarded for it in next year's contract.

I must have been asked ten thousand times how much I would be worth in today's market. I don't know, but I like what Joe DiMaggio said when he was asked the same question.

"I'd walk into the owner's office to talk contract," Joe said, "and I'd say, 'Hi ya, partner.'"

Times sure have changed. Players today are getting multiyear contracts for $3 million a year, sometimes $4 million! When I played, it was the ballplayers who were dumb.

But I don't begrudge the players of today. They deserve to get whatever they can get. For so many years, players were like second-class citizens, forced to accept whatever the owner or general manager wanted to pay them. Maybe it's gone a little too far in the other direction, but I'm glad to see ballplayers finally getting their due.

I don't begrudge them and I don't regret anything about my baseball career, except maybe all the injuries I had and all my strikeouts. But it was a good life, and it's still paying off. Everything I have today, I owe to baseball.

Players today make more money, but I don't think they have as much fun as we did. They don't seem to have the camaraderie and the good times we had. In my day, we were more like family. We hung around together in groups, went out together, spent a lot of time together. You don't see very much of that these days. For one thing, the players don't have roommates anymore. Every player is entitled to his own room, if he wants it. I was one of the first to get my own room, but Whitey and I would always get adjoining rooms and open the door between us and it was just like we were roommates sharing a suite.

Another thing: players don't seem to talk baseball as much today as we did. They don't sit in hotel lobbies like we did. They'll go to their rooms and watch television, or they'll go out making appearances, or they'll stay in their room studying the stock market. When ball clubs traveled by train, ballplayers would spend a lot of time with each other, playing cards or just talking baseball. That's changed. I'm not saying it was better back then, it just was different.

I'm not sure I'd want to be a player today. Except for the money, of course. Everything else, I wouldn't want to change. I played eighteen seasons, appeared in twelve World Series, was on the winning side in seven of them, set a few records, made the Hall of Fame and was the last player to lead the major leagues in batting average, home runs and runs batted in all in the same year, 1956. A year I'll never forget. My favorite summer.

CHASING RUTH

HOMER	DATE	PITCHER, TEAM	SITE	MEN ON
1	April 17	Camilo Pascual, Washington	Wash.	0
2	April 17	Camilo Pascual, Washington	Wash.	2
3	April 20	Ike Delock, Boston	N.Y.	2
4	April 21	George Susce, Boston	N.Y.	1
5	May 1	Steve Gromek, Detroit	N.Y.	0
6	May 2	Frank Lary, Detroit	N.Y.	0
7	May 3	Art Ceccarelli, Kansas City	N.Y.	0
8	May 5	Lou Kretlow, Kansas City	N.Y.	1
9	May 5	Moe Burtschy, Kansas City	N.Y.	0
10	May 8	Early Wynn, Cleveland	N.Y.	0
11	May 10	Bob Lemon, Cleveland	N.Y.	0
12	May 15	Bob Lemon, Cleveland	Cleve.	0
13	May 16	Bud Daley, Cleveland	Cleve.	0
14	May 18	Billy Pierce, Chicago	Chic.	1
15	May 18	Dixie Howell, Chicago	Chic.	0
16	May 21	Moe Burtschy, Kansas City	K.C.	0
17	May 24	Duke Maas, Detroit	Det.	0

HOMER	DATE	PITCHER, TEAM	SITE	MEN ON
18	May 29	Willard Nixon, Boston	N.Y.	1
19	May 30	Pedro Ramos, Washington	N.Y.	2
20	May 30	Camilo Pascual, Washington	N.Y.	0
21	June 6	Lou Kretlow, Kansas City	N.Y.	1
22	June 14	Jim Wilson, Chicago	N.Y.	0
23	June 15	Mike Garcia, Cleveland	Cleve.	1
24	June 16	Herb Score, Cleveland	Cleve.	1
25	June 18	Paul Foytack, Detroit	Det.	2
26	June 20	Billy Hoeft, Detroit	Det.	0
27	June 20	Billy Hoeft, Detroit	Det.	0
28	July 1	Dean Stone, Washington	N.Y.	0
29	July 1	Bud Byerly, Washington	N.Y.	1
30	July 14	Herb Score, Cleveland	N.Y.	0
31	July 18	Paul Foytack, Detroit	N.Y.	0
32	July 22	Art Ditmar, Kansas City	N.Y.	1
33	July 30	Bob Lemon, Cleveland	Cleve.	3
34	July 30	Bob Feller, Cleveland	Cleve.	1
35	August 4	Virgil Trucks, Detroit	Det.	1
36	August 4	Virgil Trucks, Detroit	Det.	0
37	August 5	Jim Bunning, Detroit	Det.	0
38	August 8	Camilo Pascual, Washington	Wash.	1
39	August 9	Hal Griggs, Washington	Wash.	1
40	August 11	Hal Brown, Baltimore	N.Y.	2

HOMER	DATE	PITCHER, TEAM	SITE	MEN ON
41	August 12	Don Ferrarese, Baltimore	N.Y.	1
42	August 14	Mel Parnell, Boston	N.Y.	1
43	August 23	Paul LaPalme, Chicago	N.Y.	0
44	August 25	Dick Donovan, Chicago	N.Y.	1
45	August 28	Art Ditmar, Kansas City	N.Y.	2
46	August 29	Jack McMahan, Kansas City	N.Y.	0
47	August 31	Camilo Pascual, Washington	Wash.	0
48	Sept. 13	Tom Gorman, Kansas City	K.C.	0
49	Sept. 16	Early Wynn, Cleveland	Cleve.	0
50	Sept. 18	Billy Pierce, Chicago	Chic.	0
51	Sept. 21	Frank Sullivan, Boston	Boston	0
52	Sept. 28	Bob Porterfield, Boston	N.Y.	0